Be prepared...
To learn...
To succeed...

D1710580

Get **REA**dy. It all starts here. REA's preparation for the Ohio Graduation Test is **fully aligned** with the Academic Content Standards of the Ohio Department of Education.

Free!
2 Practice Tests Online
www.rea.com/OGT

Visit us online at www.rea.com

Ready, Set, Go!®

OGT

Mathematics

3rd Edition

Staff of Research & Education Association

 Research & Education Association

The standards presented in this book were created and implemented by the Ohio Department of Education (ODE). For further information, visit the ODE website at *www.ode.state.oh.us/proficiency*.

Research & Education Association
61 Ethel Road West
Piscataway, New Jersey 08854
E-mail: info@rea.com

Ready, Set, Go!®
Ohio Graduation Test in Mathematics

Printed in the United States of America

Library of Congress Control Number 2010937209

ISBN 13: 978-0-7386-0942-3
ISBN 10: 0-7386-0942-0

About Research & Education Association

Founded in 1959, Research & Education Association is dedicated to publishing the finest and most effective educational materials—including software, study guides, and test preps—for students in middle school, high school, college, graduate school, and beyond. Today REA's wide-ranging catalog is a leading resource for teachers, students, and professionals. We invite you to visit us at *www.rea.com* to find out how REA is making the world smarter.

Acknowledgments

We would like to thank REA's Larry B. Kling, Vice President, Editorial, for supervising development; Pam Weston, Publisher, for setting the quality standards for production integrity; Alice Leonard, Senior Editor, for project management and preflight editorial review; Christine Saul, Senior Graphic Artist, for cover design; Rachel DiMatteo, Graphic Designer, for post-production file mapping; and Caragraphics for typesetting this edition.

Contents

Introduction 1
About This Book 1
About the Test.. 1
How to Use This Book 3
Overview of the OGT in Mathematics.......................... 3
Standards 5
Test-Taking Strategies.. 9

Chapter 1: Numbers, Number Sense, and Operations, Part 1 11

Types of Numbers.. 12
Rational and Irrational Numbers 12
Absolute Value 13
Equivalent Numbers 13
Let's Review 1: Equivalent Numbers........................ 18
Powers 19
Scientific Notation.. 20
Square Roots and Radicals 22
Let's Review 2: Equivalent Numbers 24
Chapter 1 Practice Problems 26
Chapter 1 Answer Explanations................................ 30

Chapter 2: Numbers, Number Sense, and Operations, Part 2 33

Estimation.. 34
Let's Review 3: Estimation 37
Ratios 38
Proportions.. 38
Powers 39
Let's Review 4: Ratios, Proportions, and Powers 42
Computing Money Problems 43
Let's Review 5: Computing Money Problems............ 46
Chapter 2 Practice Problems 48
Chapter 2 Answer Explanations................................ 51

Chapter 3: Data Analysis and Probability, Part 1 57

Probability 58
Let's Review 6: Probability 60
Combinations 62
Let's Review 7: Combinations 63
Mean, Median, Mode, and Range 64
Let's Review 8: Mean, Median, Mode, and Range 66
Chapter 3 Practice Problems 68
Chapter 3 Answer Explanations 73

Chapter 4: Data Analysis and Probability, Part 2 77

Line Graphs 78
Bar Graphs 78
Circle Graphs 79
Venn Diagrams 80
Let's Review 9: Graphs 81
Scatter Plots 83
Box-and-Whisker Plots 84
Stem-and-Leaf Plots 85
Bias 86
Let's Review 10: Plots 87
Chapter 4 Practice Problems 89
Chapter 4 Answer Explanations 95

Chapter 5: Geometry and Spatial Sense, Part 1 99

Congruent Figures 99
Plane Figures 100
Three-Dimensional Figures 102
Let's Review 11: Figures 105
Lines and Angles 107
Line and Angle Relationships 109
Let's Review 12: Lines and Angles 111
Triangles 111
Pythagorean Theorem 113
Let's Review 13: Triangles 115
Chapter 5 Practice Problems 118
Chapter 5 Answer Explanations 120

Chapter 6: Geometry and Spatial Sense, Part 2 123

The Coordinate Plane 124
Let's Review 14: The Coordinate Plane 125
Transformations 128
Let's Review 15: Figure Transformations 130
Nets 131
Slope 132
Let's Review 16: Nets and Slope 133
Chapter 6 Practice Problems 135
Chapter 6 Answer Explanations 140

Chapter 7: Measurement 145

Similar Figures 146
Let's Review 17: Similar Figures 148
Perimeter 149
Circumference 150
Central Angles 151
Let's Review 18: Perimeter and Central Angles 152
Area 154
Volume 157
Surface Area 159
Multi-step Problems 160
Let's Review 19: Area and Volume 161
Chapter 7 Practice Problems 163
Chapter 7 Answer Explanations 167

Chapter 8: Patterns, Functions, and Algebra 171

Expressions 172
Equations 173
Inequalities 177
Let's Review 20: Equations and Expressions 178
Patterns 181
Linear Equations 182
Functional Relationships 183
Let's Review 21: Linear Equations and Functional Relationships 187
Inverse Relationships 192
Rate of Change 192

Let's Review 22: Rate of Change 193

Quadratic Functions 194

Quadratic Equations 196

Let's Review 23: Quadratic Equations 196

Chapter 8 Practice Problems 199

Chapter 8 Answer Explanations 203

Practice Test 1 207

Practice Test 1 Answer Explanations 232

Practice Test 2 239

Practice Test 2 Answer Explanations 267

Optional Graph Paper 273

Answer Document: Practice Test 1 274

Optional Graph Paper 283

Answer Document: Practice Test 2 284

Index 299

Introduction

Passing the OGT Mathematics Test

About This Book

REA's Ohio Graduation Test (OGT) Mathematics book is an accurate and comprehensive guide aligned with the Academic Content Standards of the Ohio Department of Education. Inside you will find chapters designed to equip you with the information and strategies needed to prepare for and pass the test. The standards covered are listed at the beginning of each chapter.

We provide you with a total of four full-length practice tests—two at the end of this book and two online—each of which is based on the official OGT. The online tests can be found on our website at www.rea.com/OGT. The practice tests contain every type of question that you can expect to encounter on the OGT. At the end of the book, you will find an answer key with detailed explanations designed to help you completely understand the content upon which your success on the test depends.

About the Test

Who Takes These Tests and What Are They Used For?

The five parts of the Ohio Graduation Tests are aligned to Ohio's academic content standards in mathematics, writing, reading, science, and social studies, which were adopted by the State Board of Education.

The graduating class of 2007 was the first class responsible for taking the OGT and passing all five tests* as a graduation requirement. Students must pass these tests in order to earn an Ohio high-school diploma. Students in grades 3 through 8 take Achievement Tests.

Is There a Registration Fee?

No.

When and Where Is the Test Given?

Students take the OGT for the first time in the spring of their sophomore year. If they do not pass, students can continue to take the tests in the fall and spring of their junior and senior years, and in the summer. The OGT is administered as follows:

- Spring of 10th grade
- Summer between 10th and 11th grade (optional)
- Fall and spring of 11th grade
- Summer between 11th and 12th grade (optional)
- Fall and spring of 12th grade

Tests are given in school. Students have up to two-and-a-half hours to take each of the tests.

Test Accommodations and Special Situations

Federal law requires every student to take the OGT or an alternate assessment. Every effort is made for students with disabilities seeking a standard high school diploma to take the OGT. Students whose Individual Education Plan (IEP) excuses them from having to pass the OGT to graduate may be awarded a diploma. Students who have an IEP that requires a different test can take an alternate assessment of the

*Some exceptions apply. Please see *www.ohiostudents.com* for details.

OGT. Students whose primary language is not English must achieve passing scores on the OGT in order to be awarded a diploma. However, bilingual forms of the OGT are available. English audio CD-ROMs, large-print formats, and oral translation scripts are also available to those requiring such accommodations.

Additional Information and Support

Additional resources to help you prepare to take the OGT can be found on the Ohio Department of Education Web site at *http://www.ode.state.oh.us.*

How to Use This Book

What Do I Study First?

Read over the review sections and the suggestions for test taking. Studying the review sections thoroughly will reinforce the basic skills needed to do well on the test. Be sure to take the practice tests to become familiar with the format and procedures involved in taking the actual OGT.

When Should I Start Studying?

It is never too early to start studying for the OGT. The earlier you begin, the more time you will have to sharpen your skills. Do not procrastinate! Cramming is *not* an effective way to study because it does not allow you the time needed to learn the test material. The sooner you learn the format of the exam, the more time you will have to familiarize yourself with the exam content.

Overview of the OGT in Mathematics

The 44 questions on the mathematics portion of the OGT are based on five broad strands, or standards, as follows:

1. Number, Number Sense, and Operations (approximately 15% of the test)

2. Measurement (approximately 15% of the test)

3. Geometry and Spatial Sense (approximately 20% of the test)

4. Patterns, Functions, and Algebra (approximately 25% of the test)

5. Data Analysis and Probability (approximately 25% of the test)

The test consists of 32 multiple-choice items, 5 short-answer items, and 1 extended-response item. In addition, there are six experimental questions. These are unscored. You will not know which questions are unscored, so do your best on all of them. Multiple-choice items require you to select the correct response from a list of four options. Short-answer and extended-response items require you to generate a written response. A short-answer item requires a brief response, usually a few sentences or a numeric solution to a straightforward problem. An extended-response item requires you to solve a more complex problem or task and to provide a more in-depth response. The questions typically ask you to show your work or calculations, explain your reasoning, and justify the procedures you used.

Short-answer items may each take up to five minutes to complete, and responses receive a score of 0, 1, or 2 points. Extended-response items may each require 5 to 15 minutes to complete, and responses receive a score of 0, 1, 2, 3, or 4 points.

Brief descriptions of the levels of complexity used in item development include the following:

- **Low Complexity:** Items rely heavily on recall and recognition of facts, definitions and procedures. Items typically specify what the students are to do and often involve carrying out a specified, routing, procedure. (Approximately 25% of the items)

- **Moderate Complexity:** Items require more interpretation of a problem or situation and choice among alternative solution strategies than low complexity items. Students are expected to make decisions about what to do, using informal reasoning and problem-solving strategies. The solution process ordinarily requires more than one step. (Approximately 50% of the items)

- **High Complexity:** Items require more sophisticated analysis, planning, and reasoning in more complex or non-routine problem situations. Students are often asked to think in an abstract or sophisticated way and to justify their reasoning and solution process. (Approximately 25% of the items)

Benchmarks by Standard*

Numbers, Number Sense, and Operations

A. Use scientific notation to express large numbers and numbers less than one.

B. Identify subsets of the real number system.

C. Apply properties of operations and the real number system, and justify when they hold for a set of numbers.

D. Connect physical, verbal, and symbolic representations of integers, rational numbers, and irrational numbers.

E. Compare, order and determine equivalent forms of real numbers.

F. Explain the effects of operations on the magnitude of quantities.

G. Estimate, compute, and solve problems involving real numbers, including ratio, proportion, and percent, and explain solutions.

H. Find the square root of perfect squares, and approximate the square root of non-perfect squares.

I. Estimate, compute, and solve problems involving scientific notation, square roots, and numbers with integer exponents.

*by the end of the 8–10 program

Data Analysis and Probability

A. Create, interpret, and use graphical displays and statistical measures to describe data; e.g., box-and-whiskers plots, histograms, scatterplots, measures of center and variability.

B. Evaluate different graphical representations of the same data to determine which is the most appropriate representation for an identified purpose.

C. Compare the characteristics of the mean, median, and mode for a given set of data, and explain which measure of center best represents the data.

D. Find, use, and interpret measures of center and spread, such as mean and quartiles, and use those measures to compare and draw conclusions about sets of data.

E. Evaluate the validity of claims and predictions that are based on data by examining the appropriateness of the data collection and analysis.

F. Construct convincing arguments based on analysis of data and interpretation of graphs.

G. Describe sampling methods and analyze the effects of method chosen on how well the resulting sample represents the population.

H. Use counting techniques, such as permutations and combinations, to determine the total number of options and possible outcomes.

I. Design an experiment to test a theoretical probability, and record and explain the results.

J. Compute probabilities of compound events, independent events, and simple dependent events.

K. Make predictions based on theoretical probabilities and experimental results.

Measurement

A. Solve increasingly complex non-routine measurement problems and check for reasonableness of results.

B. Use formulas to find surface area and volume for specified three-dimensional objects accurate to a specified level of precision.

C. Apply indirect measurement techniques, tools, and formulas, as appropriate, to find perimeter, circumference and area of circles, triangles, quadrilaterals, and composite shapes, and to find volumes of prisms, cylinders, and pyramids.

D. Use proportional reasoning and apply indirect measurement techniques, including right triangle trigonometry and properties of similar triangles, to solve problems involving measurements and rates.

E. Estimate and compute various attributes, including length, angle measure, area, surface area, and volume, to a specified level or precision.

F. Write and solve real-word, multi-step problems involving money, elapsed time and temperature, and verify reasonableness of solutions.

Geometry and Spatial Sense

A. Formally define geometric figures.

B. Describe and apply the properties of similar and congruent figures; and justify conjectures involving similarity and congruence.

C. Recognize and apply angle relationships in situations involving intersecting lines, perpendicular lines, and parallel lines.

D. Use coordinate geometry to represent and examine the properties of geometric figures.

E. Draw and construct representations of two- and three-dimensional geometric objects using a variety of tools, such as a straightedge, compass, and technology.

F. Represent and model transformations in a coordinate plane and describe the results.

G. Prove or disprove conjectures and solve problems involving two- and three-dimensional objects represented within a coordinate system.

H. Establish the validity of conjectures about geometric objects, their properties and relationships by counter-example, inductive and deductive reasoning, and critiquing arguments made by others.

I. Use right triangle trigonometric relationships to determine lengths and angle measures.

Patterns, Functions, and Algebra

A. Generalize and explain patterns and sequences in order to find the next term and the nth term.

B. Identify and classify functions as linear or nonlinear, and contrast their properties using tables, graphs, or equations.

C. Translate information from one representation (words, table, graph, or equation) to another representation of a relation or function.

D. Use algebraic representations, such as tables, graphs, expressions, functions, and inequalities, to model and solve problem situations.

E. Analyze and compare functions and their graphs using attributes, such as rates of change, intercepts, and zeros.

F. Solve and graph linear equations and inequalities.

G. Solve quadratic equations with real roots by graphing, formula, and factoring.

H. Solve systems of linear equations involving two variables graphically and symbolically.

I. Model and solve problem situations involving direct and inverse variation.

J. Describe and interpret rates of change from graphical and numerical data.

Test-Taking Strategies

What to Do before the Test

- **Pay attention in class.**

- **Carefully work through the chapters of this book.** Mark any topics that you find difficult, so that you can focus on them while studying and get extra help if necessary.

- **Take the practice tests and become familiar with the format of the OGT.** When you are practicing, simulate the conditions under which you will be taking the actual test. Stay calm and pace yourself. After simulating the test only a couple of times, you will feel more confident, and this will boost your chances of doing well.

- **Students who have difficulty concentrating or taking tests in general may have severe test anxiety.** Tell your parents, a teacher, a counselor, the school nurse, or a school psychologist well in advance of the test if this applies to you. They may be able to give you some useful strategies that will help you feel more relaxed and then be able to do your best on the test.

What to Do during the Test

- **Read all of the possible answers.** Even if you think you have found the correct response, do not automatically assume that it is the best answer. Read through each answer choice to be sure that you are not making a mistake by jumping to conclusions.

- **Use the process of elimination.** Go through each answer to a question and eliminate as many of the answer choices as possible. By eliminating two answer choices, you have given yourself a better chance of getting the item correct, because there will only be two choices left from which to make your selection. Sometimes a question will have one or two answer choices that are a little odd. These answers will be obviously wrong for one of several reasons: they may be impossible given the conditions of the problem, they may violate mathematical rules or principles, or they may be illogical.

- **Work on the easier questions first.** If you find yourself working too long on one question, make a mark next to it in your test booklet and continue. After you have answered all of the questions that you know, go back to the ones you have skipped.

- **Be sure that the answer oval you are marking corresponds to the number of the question in the test booklet.** The multiple-choice sections are graded by machine, so marking one wrong answer can throw off your answer key and your score. Be extremely careful.

- **Work from answer choices.** You can use a multiple-choice format to your advantage by working backward from the answer choices to solve a problem. This strategy can be helpful if you can just plug the answers into a given formula or equation. You may be able to make a better choice on a difficult problem if you eliminate choices that you know do not fit into the problem.

- **If you cannot determine what the correct answer is, answer the question anyway.** The OGT does not subtract points for wrong answers, so be sure to fill in an answer for every question. It works to your advantage because you could guess correctly and increase your score.

Chapter 1

Numbers, Number Sense, and Operations, Part 1

$$3+7<16$$
$$\sqrt{8^2+5}$$
$$20-9\times6$$

Benchmarks

A. Use scientific notation to express large numbers and numbers less than one.

B. Identify subsets of the real number system.

C. Apply properties of operations and the real number system, and justify when they hold for a set of numbers.

D. Connect physical, verbal and symbolic representations of integers, rational numbers, and irrational numbers.

E. Compare, order, and determine equivalent forms of real numbers.

The standards on the OGT require you to understand that there are different kinds of numbers. For example, you need to know the difference between a rational and an irrational number. You also need to be able to determine the value of numbers expressed in different ways. You should be able to compare decimals and fractions to determine which is greater. You will learn these skills in this chapter.

Scientific notation is a shorthand way of writing very large or very small numbers. You will also learn about scientific notation and other numbers with exponents in this chapter.

Types of Numbers

Integers are whole numbers, as are their opposites. A number's opposite is its negative. The numbers below are pairs of opposites:

Number	Opposite
1	−1
2	−2
3	−3
4	−4
5	−5

Real numbers are numbers that can be placed on a number line such as the one shown below.

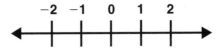

Rational and Irrational Numbers

Real numbers are grouped into two categories: rational and irrational. A **rational number** is a number that can be written as a fraction and can be placed on a number line. All whole numbers are rational numbers. For example, 7 is a rational number because it can be written as $\frac{7}{1}$. Negative numbers are rational numbers. Terminating decimals, which are decimals that "end," and repeating decimals such as $0.33\overline{3}$ are also rational numbers. For example, the decimal 0.2 can be written as the fraction $\frac{2}{10}$, and $0.33\overline{3}$ can be written as the fraction $\frac{1}{3}$, so these decimals are rational numbers.

In contrast, **irrational numbers** cannot be expressed as fractions. When irrational numbers are expressed as decimals, they do not repeat in a logical pattern or terminate. They keep on going forever without a repeating pattern. For example, $\sqrt{2}$ is an irrational number. Expressed as a decimal, $\sqrt{2}$ is 1.414213562…. It keeps on going forever, but the digits do not repeat. These numbers also are irrational:

2.3459564646332…

0.999088432…

π

Absolute Value

The **absolute value** of a number is the number of units it is from 0 on the number line. It is always a positive number. To find a number's absolute value, it helps to imagine a number line such as the one shown at the beginning of this chapter. You can see that the absolute value of -2 is 2 because -2 is 2 units from 0. Some questions on the OGT may ask you to find the absolute value of a number.

Equivalent Numbers

Numbers that are said to be **equivalent** have the same value. With some numbers, it is easy to see that they are equivalent. For example, you know that $\frac{7}{1} = 7$, and you probably know that $\frac{5}{5}$ is equivalent to 1.

Determining whether numbers are equivalent when they are in different forms is more difficult, however. You might not know right away that 8^3 is equivalent to 512.

The best way to determine whether numbers are equivalent is put them into the same form. The following guidelines can help you to do this.

Fractions

A **fraction** represents the number of parts of a whole thing. The whole is divided into an equal number of parts, and the denominator (bottom number of a fraction) tells how many parts make up the whole. The numerator (top number) of a fraction tells how many of these parts you have. For example, the fraction $\frac{2}{3}$ tells you that you have 2 out of the 3 equal parts.

If the denominators of two fractions are the same, the fraction with the *larger* numerator is the larger fraction. For example, $\frac{3}{7}$ is larger than $\frac{2}{7}$.

Equivalent fractions have the same value and represent the same part of a whole. For example, $\frac{1}{2}$ is equivalent to $\frac{2}{4}$ and $\frac{3}{6}$. If two fractions have different numerators and denominators, you can determine whether they are equivalent by making the denominators the same. To do this, you must realize that 1 times any number equals the same number.

Multiply the fractions by the equivalent of 1 (such as $\frac{2}{2}$ or $\frac{4}{4}$) so that the denominators of the two fractions are the same. Often only one fraction needs to be changed for the denominators to be the same. Compare the results to see whether the fractions are equivalent. By comparing numerators (if the denominators are the same), you can tell which of two fractions is larger.

To multiply two fractions, multiply the two numerators to get the new numerator, and then multiply the two denominators to get the new denominator, so $\frac{2}{5} \times \frac{3}{4} = \frac{6}{20}$.

Therefore, to see whether $\frac{1}{2}$ and $\frac{2}{4}$ are equivalent, multiply $\frac{1}{2}$ by $\frac{2}{2}$ (which equals 1). Then, $\frac{1}{2} \times \frac{2}{2} = \frac{2}{4}$. The two fractions are equivalent.

Let's try another example.

Are $\frac{2}{3}$ and $\frac{4}{5}$ equivalent?

In this case, multiply $\frac{2}{3}$ by $\frac{5}{5}$ and multiply $\frac{4}{5}$ by $\frac{3}{3}$, so they will both have denominators of 15:

$$\frac{2}{3} \times \frac{5}{5} = \frac{10}{15}$$

$$\frac{4}{5} \times \frac{3}{3} = \frac{12}{15}$$

The fractions are not equivalent. In fact, you can see that $\frac{4}{5}$ is larger than $\frac{2}{3}$.

If you're asked to compare two or more mixed numbers (a mixed number has a whole number and a fraction, such as $1\frac{1}{2}$), the one with the larger whole number is the greater number. For example:

$2\frac{1}{3}$ is greater than $1\frac{1}{3}$. You don't even have to compare the fractional parts, unless the whole numbers are the same.

If the whole number parts are the same, use the method you just learned to compare the fractional parts to determine which mixed number is larger.

Decimals

A mixed decimal number, such as 3.14, includes a decimal point and has two parts. The part to the left of the decimal point is a whole number, and the part to the right of the decimal point, including the decimal point, is called a **decimal**. A decimal is a portion of a whole number, and has a value less than 1. Therefore, the number 3 is greater than the number .33. Note that the decimal .33 can also be written as 0.33, indicating that there is no whole number part to the decimal.

The decimal system is based on the number 10. (This probably has to do with the fact that most humans have 10 fingers.) Each digit in a decimal number has a value assigned to its "place." To the left of the decimal point, the digits in the whole number appear as you are used to seeing them (ones, tens, hundreds, etc.), but to the right of the decimal point they are, (from left to right), tenths, hundredths, thousandths, etc. (The decimal system is discussed further in the section on scientific notation later in this chapter.)

So for the decimal number 4.25, the 4 is a whole number, the 2 is tenths and the 5 is hundredths. You could put these last two digits together and say 25 hundredths. So you would read 4.25 as "four point two five," or "four and twenty five hundredths."

Do you know which is greater, .334 or .3? To determine which decimal is greater, align the decimal points vertically, like this:

.334
.3

Then fill in the empty place values with zeros so both numbers have the same number of digits before you do the comparison:

.334

.300

Which decimal is greater? If you said .334, you're correct! This method is similar to comparing whole numbers, but you must remember to add the zeros to the ends of the decimals so that each decimal has the same number of digits.

If you're asked to compare two mixed decimals, the number with the greater whole number part is always larger, just as it was for mixed fractions. For example, 2.334 is greater than 1.945. To compare two mixed decimals that have the same whole number, use the method you just learned to compare the decimal parts to determine which is greater.

For example, to compare 1.4 and 1.36, align the decimal points of the numbers vertically and fill in zeros if necessary:

1.40

1.36

Now you can see that 1.4 is definitely greater.

Percents

A **percent** has a percent sign (%) and refers to how much of 100 a number is. For example, 75% means 75 out of 100.

Determining which of two (or more) percents is greater is sometimes easy. For example, 75% is obviously greater than 65%. Determining which number in a different form is equivalent to or greater than a percentage, however, is a little more difficult. For example, it is not immediately obvious whether 75% is equivalent to $\frac{3}{4}$. (It is!)

As you learned earlier in this chapter, to find an equivalent number or to compare numbers, you must convert the numbers to the same form. Usually, it is easiest to convert numbers of different forms into decimals to do this comparison.

To convert a percent into a decimal, move the decimal point to the left two places. (These places represent the two zeros in 100.) Look at the following examples:

$$32\% = .32$$
$$75\% = .75$$
$$210\% = 2.10$$

Fill in with zeros if necessary:

$$5\% = .05$$
$$.3\% = .003$$

Now, suppose you want to convert a decimal to a percent. Then you would move the decimal point two places to the *right*, and add the percentage sign.

$$.20 = 20\%$$

If you need to convert a percent to a fraction, put the percentage over 100. Then **reduce the fraction**, if possible, by the following method: Think of a number that divides evenly into both the numerator and denominator (called a common factor). Do that division, and the results for each part give you the reduced fraction.

So for 20%, the calculation would be: $20\% = \dfrac{20}{100} = \dfrac{1}{5}$, by dividing both numerator and denominator by 20.

Let's say that you didn't recognize right off that 20 divides into both 20 and 100 in the above example, and that you thought of 10 instead. Then the calculation would be: $20\% = \dfrac{20}{100} = \dfrac{2}{10}$. Perhaps now you can see that 2 will divide into both the 2 and 10. The result will be $\dfrac{2}{10} = \dfrac{1}{5}$, the same result as when you reduced the fraction by using 20 as the common factor: $20\% = \dfrac{20}{100} = \dfrac{2}{10} = \dfrac{1}{5}$.

Let's Review 1: Equivalent Numbers

Complete each of the following questions about equivalent numbers. Use the Tip below each question to help you choose the correct answer. When you finish, check your answers at the end of this chapter.

1. **Which fraction is equal to .45?**

   A. $\dfrac{1}{45}$

   B. $\dfrac{9}{20}$

   C. $\dfrac{1}{4}$

   D. $\dfrac{1}{2}$

TIP

Find the decimal equivalent of each fraction or change .45 to a fraction.

2. **Which number is irrational?**

   A. $\sqrt{3}$

   B. $\dfrac{35}{4}$

   C. 1

   D. -5

TIP

Choose the number that cannot be expressed as a fraction and that does not terminate when expressed as a decimal. If you aren't sure, reread the section about rational and irrational numbers.

3. **Which expression is *not* equivalent to 6?**

   A. $|-6|$

   B. 6^1

   C. $\sqrt{36}$

   D. $\dfrac{6}{36}$

TIP

Determine the value of each answer choice. Choose the answer choice that does not equal 6.

Powers

The **power** (indicated by a raised number, called an **exponent**) tells you how many times a number appears when it is multiplied by itself. Thus, the first power of any number is equal to itself. For example,

$$8^1 = 8$$

When you raise a number to the second power, you **square** the number. When you square a number, you multiply it by itself, as in this example:

$$8^2 = 8 \times 8$$

Note that 8 appears two times in the multiplication, and two is the exponent.

When you raise a number to the third power, you **cube** the number. To cube a number, multiply it by itself and then by itself again:

$$8^3 = 8 \times 8 \times 8$$

You can keep raising numbers to higher and higher powers, as in this example:

$8^9 = 8 \times 8 \times 8 \times 8 \times 8 \times 8 \times 8 \times 8 \times 8$, where the number 8 appears nine times.

You are allowed to use a calculator on the OGT. To square a number, press AC. Then press the number and the x^2 key. For numbers raised to a higher power, press AC. Then press the number, and then the x^y key, and then the exponent (y). For example, to determine 5^3, press AC$-5-x^y-3$. Use your calculator to raise each of the numbers in the left column below to the indicated power. See if you get the answers shown in the right column.

$15^2 = 225$	
$16^1 = 16$	
$8^4 = 4{,}096$	
$20^2 = 400$	
$9^5 = 59{,}049$	

Scientific Notation

Scientific notation is a type of shorthand for writing numbers that are very large or very small. These numbers contain many zeros. The table below shows the powers of 10 used in scientific notation. (Note that for powers of 10, the exponent tells you how many zeros follow the "1.")

Number Value	Power of 10
1	10^0
10	10^1
100	10^2
1.000	10^3
10.000	10^4
100,000	10^5
1000,000	10^6

But what about a number such as 2,500,000? You would write this number in scientific notation. Move the decimal point to the *left* until there is just one digit to the left of it. Here you would move the decimal point until it is between the 2 and the 5. The number of places you move the decimal point (in this case, 6) is the exponent of 10.

$$2{,}\overset{\longleftarrow}{500{,}000} = 2.5 \times 10^6$$

Let's try another number. How would you write 32,000 in scientific notation? Remember to move the decimal point until it is in between the 3 and the 2. The number of places you moved it is the exponent of 10.

$$32{,}000 = 3.2 \times 10^4$$

Now, let's work backwards. Write out the number 4.8×10^5.

This time you need to move the decimal point to the *right* five places. Remember to fill in zeros.

$$4.8 \times 10^5 = 480{,}000$$

When you work with large numbers on a calculator, the calculator automatically writes the number in scientific notation if there are too many zeros to display. Scientific notation on a calculator looks different, however, because a calculator omits the "$\times 10$". For example, 2,400,000 might appear as 2.4E6, meaning 2.4×10^6.

Very small numbers (decimals) can also be represented with scientific notation, but in a slightly different way. A negative exponent is used with the number 10 to indicate a decimal.

The following table shows how scientific notation is used to represent very small numbers. (Note that for negative powers of 10, the exponent tells you what "place" the 1 is in, counting to the right from the decimal point.)

Decimal	Power
0.1	10^{-1}
0.01	10^{-2}
0.001	10^{-3}
0.0001	10^{-4}
0.00001	10^{-5}
0.000001	10^{-6}

How do you think you would write 0.0062 using scientific notation? This time, you would move the decimal point to the *right* until it has only one non-zero digit before it. Here you would move the decimal point until it is between the 6 and the 2. You would need to move it three places, so your exponent would be -3.

$$0.0062 = 6.2 \times 10^{-3}$$

Square Roots and Radicals

The **square root** of a number is the **inverse operation** (opposite) of squaring the number (multiplying the number by itself). For example, $\sqrt{144} = 12$ because $12^2 = 144$.

Not every number is a perfect square, however. This means you might not always get a whole number when you find the square root. For example,

$$\sqrt{3} = 1.73205081$$

Radicals are symbols for roots, such as the square root of 9, $\sqrt{9}$. Radical signs can also have indexes within them, such as $\sqrt[3]{27}$, and $\sqrt[4]{16}$, which stand for the cube root of 27, which is 3, and the fourth root of 16, which is 2. Square roots would have a 2 as an index, but this is usually omitted, so $\sqrt{25} = 5$.

Sometimes a coefficient appears before a radical. For example $3\sqrt{5}$ means "3 times the square root of 5." When *adding or subtracting* radicals, be sure the number under the square root sign (called the **radicand**) is the same, and add or subtract the coefficients. For example,

$$2\sqrt{3} + 6\sqrt{3} = 8\sqrt{3}$$

When *multiplying or dividing* radicals, the radicands need not be the same. Follow the same rules as you would when multiplying or dividing whole numbers. Treat the coefficients and radicals separately. For example,

$$\sqrt{3} \times \sqrt{3} = \sqrt{9}$$
$$\sqrt{8} \times \sqrt{2} = \sqrt{16}$$
$$3\sqrt{2} \times 4\sqrt{5} = 12\sqrt{10}$$

You can use your calculator to quickly find the square root of a number on the OGT. Press the square root key ($\sqrt{\ }$), then the number and then the $=$ key. For example, to find the square root of 169, press the $\sqrt{\ }$ key, then $1-6-9$, then $=$. The answer will be 13.

Let's Review 2: Equivalent Numbers

Complete each of the following questions about equivalent numbers. Use the Tip below each question to help you choose the correct answer. When you finish, check your answers at the end of this chapter.

1. **Which is another way to express 144?**

   A. 12^2

   B. 4^4

   C. 14.4×10^2

   D. 8^3

TIP

If you're not sure of the correct answer, begin by eliminating those that you know are incorrect.

2. **The population of Ohio is about 11 million. What is 11 million expressed in scientific notation?**

   A. 1.1×10^8

   B. 1.1×10^7

   C. 1.1×10^6

   D. 1.1×10^5

TIP

Write out 11 million as a number. Remember that with scientific notation, count the number of places you must move the decimal in the number when it is written out to get to 1.1. The number of places you moved the decimal is the exponent of 10.

3. The side of a right triangle is $\sqrt{32}$ inches. Which point is closest to $\sqrt{32}$ on the number line?

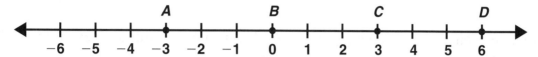

A. A

B. B

C. C

D. D

TIP

Find the square root of 32. Then choose the point that is closest to this number.

4. Which expression represents 320,000 written in scientific notation?

A. 320×10^4

B. 32×10^4

C. 3.2×10^5

D. 0.32×10^6

TIP

Remember that you have to move the decimal point until it is between the 3 and 2. The number of places you moved it is the power of 10.

5. Which expression represents .45000000 written in scientific notation?

A. 4.5×10^{-1}

B. 4.5×10^1

C. 45×10^{-2}

D. 4.5×10^2

TIP

This time you are moving the decimal to the right, so the exponent of 10 should be negative.

Chapter 1 Practice Problems

Complete each of the following practice problems. Check your answers at the end of this chapter. Be sure to read the answer explanations!

1. **Which value is the greatest?**

A. 7^3

B. 7^4

C. 8^6

D. 9^5

2. **Which answer is .64 written as a percent?**

A. .64%

B. 6.4%

C. 64%

D. 640%

3. **Which number is not equivalent to 12?**

A. $\sqrt{144}$

B. $|-12|$

C. 12^1

D. $\dfrac{12}{12}$

4. **Which expression represents 74,000 written in scientific notation?**

A. 7.4×10^{-3}

B. 7.4×10^{-4}

C. 7.4×10^{3}

D. 7.4×10^{4}

5. **Which of the numbers below is the greatest?**

A. $\sqrt{121}$

B. $\dfrac{121}{12}$

C. 1.21×10^{3}

D. 12% of 121

6. **An architect found, on a blueprint, that the height of a doorway was to be $\sqrt{50}$ feet. Which point is closest to $\sqrt{50}$ on the number line?**

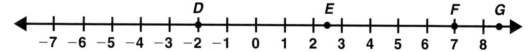

A. *D*

B. *E*

C. *F*

D. *G*

7. **Three different opinion polls show different results for the proportion of voters expected to vote for Candidate A in an election for school board members.**

   Poll 1: Eight out of every 25 voters are expected to vote for Candidate A.

   Poll 2: The percentage of voters expected to vote for Candidate A is 58%.

Poll 3: There are 120,000 people expected to vote, and of these, 45,000 are expected to vote for Candidate A.

Determine which of these polls shows the greatest favorable result for Candidate A.

8. **A building contractor is using a wire and a pulley to lift materials to the roof of a building.**

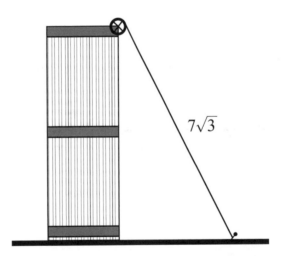

The contractor used the Pythagorean theorem to determine that the length of the wire is $7\sqrt{3}$. Which of the following numbers is closest to the length of the wire?

A.   12 feet

B.   18 feet

C.   21 feet

D.   28 feet

9. **Which number is irrational?**

A. -1

B. $\sqrt{9}$

C. $\dfrac{25}{9}$

D. $\sqrt{6}$

10. **Which point on this number line is closest to $\sqrt{5}$: *F*, *G*, *H*, or *I*?**

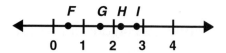

A. *F*

B. *G*

C. *H*

D. *I*

Chapter 1 Answer Explanations

Let's Review 1: Equivalent Numbers

1. B
You can answer this question two different ways. You can use your calculator to divide the denominator of each fraction into the numerator. You can also answer this problem by converting .45 into a fraction. To do this, move the decimal point two places to the right and put 45 over 100. Then reduce the fraction (the common factor is 5).

2. A
The square root of 3 doesn't terminate and doesn't repeat, so this number is irrational.

3. D
The fraction $\frac{6}{36}$ is not equivalent to the number 6, but rather the fraction $\frac{1}{6}$.

Let's Review 2: Equivalent Numbers

1. A
If you press the square root key on your calculator and then the numbers 1–4–4, you'll see that the square root of 144 is 12. So, 12^2 is the correct answer. Or you can see that A is the correct answer by pressing the x^2 key and then 1–2, which will give you 144.

2. B
You need to move the decimal point in 11,000,000 seven places to get to 1.1.

3. D
If you press the square root key on your calculator and then the numbers 3–2, you'll see that the square root of 32 is 5.65. Point D is closest to 5.65.

4. C

You need to move the decimal point 5 places to the left to get to 3.2, so the exponent of 10 is 5.

5. A

You need to move the decimal point 1 place to the right, so the exponent of 10 is –1.

Chapter 1 Practice Problems

1. C

To solve this problem, you can eliminate answer choices A and B because they are obviously smaller than the numbers in answer choices C and D (the numbers as well as the exponents are smaller). Use your calculator to find the correct answer between choices C and D.

2. C

Remember that to convert a decimal into a percent, move the decimal point two places to the right and add the percentage sign.

3. D

The value of $\frac{12}{12}$ is 1.

4. D

For scientific notation, you need to move the decimal point from the end of the number four places to the left to get between 7 and 4, so the exponent of 10 must be 4.

5. C

You might be able to answer this question by sight. If you move the decimal point in 1.21 three places to the right, the number is 1,210.

6. C

The square root of 50 is 7.07. Point *F* is closest to this number.

7. Sample answer:

To find this answer, you need to convert the numbers in each poll to a fraction. For poll 1, the fraction is $\frac{8}{25}$. For poll 2, the fraction is $\frac{58}{100}$ or $\frac{29}{50}$. For poll 3, $\frac{45,000}{120,000}$ is reduced to $\frac{9}{24}$. Therefore, poll 2 shows the greatest result. You can also solve this problem by converting the numbers to decimals and comparing the decimals.

8. A

The square root of 3 is about 1.7. If you multiply 7 by 1.7, you get 11.9, so 12 (choice A) is the closest number.

9. D

The square root of 6 is irrational because it is a decimal that doesn't terminate or repeat, so it cannot be represented as a fraction.

10. C

The square root of 5 is about 2.2. Point *H* is closest to this number on the number line.

Chapter 2

Numbers, Number Sense, and Operations, Part 2

$$6^2$$
$$35\%$$
$$87(3)$$
$$19x\text{-}2$$

Benchmarks

F. Explain the effects of operations on the magnitude of quantities.

G. Estimate, compute, and solve problems involving real numbers, including ratio, proportion, and percent, and explain solutions.

H. Find the square root of perfect squares, and approximate the square root of non-perfect squares.

I. Estimate, compute, and solve problems involving scientific notation, square roots, and numbers with integer exponents.

Some questions about numbers on the OGT will ask you to estimate an answer. You may be asked to choose the best approximate answer or to give an approximate answer. Most questions will be about real-life situations, such as having to estimate a discount for an item on sale. You'll learn some of the most common methods of estimation in this chapter.

In Chapter 1, you learned about scientific notation. In this chapter, you'll expand your knowledge and learn how to work with exponents. You'll also learn about ratios and proportions in this chapter.

Estimation

When you **estimate**, you find the approximate value.

Rounding

When you approximate answers, you round numbers to the same place value. When you round, numbers 0–4 get rounded down, and numbers 5–9 get rounded up, so when rounding to the nearest ten, 13 rounds to 10, and 17 rounds to 20.

For example, the following numbers are rounded to the tens place to estimate the sum:

$$12 + 19 \approx 10 + 20$$

If you add the estimations of these numbers, the answer is 30. The following numbers are rounded to the hundreds place to estimate the sum:

$$186 + 342 \approx 200 + 300$$

The estimated answer is 500. If you rounded the same numbers to the tens place, they would look like this:

$$190 + 340$$

Can you estimate this answer in your head? If not, use a calculator. The estimated answer is 530.

Now try to estimate $1{,}230 + 4{,}689$.

If these numbers are rounded to the thousands place,

$$1{,}230 + 4{,}689 \approx 1{,}000 + 5{,}000$$

The estimated answer is 6,000. If you rounded these numbers to the hundreds place, they would look like this:

$$1{,}200 + 4{,}700$$

and the estimated answer would be 5,900.

Round each of the numbers to the tens place to solve this problem:

Estimate the sum of 42, 14, 28, 23, and 29.

If you round the numbers to the tens place, they look like this:

Number	Rounded to the Tens
42	40
14	10
28	30
23	20
29	30

Now, add the rounded numbers:

$$40 + 10 + 30 + 20 + 30 = 130$$

The estimated answer is 130.

Clustering

To find the sum or difference of a group of numbers, it can help to **cluster** these numbers. This means that you add a few numbers at a time. For example, the numbers above could be added two at a time, like this:

$$40 + 10 = 50$$
$$50 + 30 = 80$$
$$80 + 20 = 100$$
$$100 + 30 = 130$$

Front-End Estimation

With **front-end estimation**, you round and add only the numbers in the leftmost place. For example, front-end estimation is used to estimate the difference or sum of the numbers below:

$$45{,}736 - 28{,}924 \approx$$
$$50{,}000 - 30{,}000 = 20{,}000$$

$$154 + 790 \approx$$
$$200 + 800 = 1{,}000$$

$$1{,}241 + 3{,}880 \approx$$
$$1{,}000 + 4{,}000 = 5{,}000$$

Use front-end estimation to solve this problem:

Estimate the difference between 2,945 and 1,523.

If you use front-end estimation, the numbers are rounded as follows:

Number	Rounded Using Front-End Estimation
2,945	3,000
1,523	2,000

Now, use the rounded numbers to estimate the difference:

$$3{,}000 - 2{,}000 = 1{,}000$$

Let's Review 3: Estimation

Complete each of the following questions. Use the Tip below each question to help you choose the correct answer. When you finish, check your answers at the end of this chapter.

1. **Estimate the sum of 32, 15, 67, 13, and 99.**

    A. 200

    B. 210

    C. 230

    D. 240

    Round the numbers to the nearest ten and add. When you round 99, you get 100.

2. **Keith is planning to buy a new stereo that costs $249.95, but is on sale for 10% off. What is the approximate amount of the discount on the stereo?**

    A. $20

    B. $25

    C. $30

    D. $35

    Round $249.95 to $250.00. Then estimate 10% of $250.00.

3. **Sarah earns $7 an hour bagging groceries at a corner store during the 10 weeks of summer vacation. If she averages 20 hours per week, what is a reasonable estimate of what Sarah will earn during the summer?**

    A. $140

    B. $170

    C. $1,400

    D. $14,000

    Find out how many hours Sarah worked per week, then multiply that by the number of weeks she worked.

4. **Estimate the difference 32,987 − 12,956.**

A. 10,000

B. 20,000

C. 30,000

D. 40,000

TIP

Round both numbers to the nearest ten thousand. Then subtract.

Ratios

A **ratio** is a way of comparing numbers. Ratios can be expressed by using a colon, as in 4 : 1, expressed as "4 to 1," or as a fraction, as in $\frac{100}{150} = \frac{2}{3}$.

Read this problem:

After taxes, Christa's paycheck is for $1,200. She puts $400 of this amount in a savings account. Write a ratio expressing the portion of Christa's paycheck that is put into a savings account.

Use the amount of Christa's paycheck as the denominator and the amount of money she puts in the savings account as the numerator. Then reduce the fraction.

$$\frac{400}{1200} = \frac{1}{3}, \text{ or } 1 : 3.$$

Proportions

Ratios that are equal are called **proportions**. For some problems, you will have to set up a proportion and find the value of an unknown variable. For example, read this problem:

Randy can type 150 words in 2 minutes. How many words can he type in 8 minutes?

To solve this problem, set up the first ratio and reduce:

$$\frac{150}{2} = \frac{75}{1}$$

Then set up the second proportion, which should be equal:

$$\frac{75}{1} = \frac{x}{8}$$

Solve for x by cross-multiplication. In cross-multiplication, multiply the top of one fraction by the bottom of the other, and set them equal. For this problem, that would give:

$$1 \times x = 8 \times 75, \text{ or}$$
$$x = 600 \text{ words}$$

Powers

In Chapter 1, you learned about powers and about scientific notation, which involved powers of 10. The **power** (indicated by a raised number, called an exponent) tells you how many times a quantity (called the **base**) appears when it is multiplied by itself. Chapter 1 explained the meaning of powers. This section explains how to add, subtract, multiply, and divide numbers raised to powers.

Thus, the first power of any number is equal to itself. For example,

$$8^1 = 8$$

When you raise a number to the second power, you **square** the number. When you square a number, you multiply it by itself, as in this example:

$$8^2 = 8 \times 8$$

When you raise a number to the third power, you cube the number. To cube a number, multiply it by itself and then by itself again:

$$8^3 = 8 \times 8 \times 8$$

You can keep raising numbers to higher and higher powers, as in this example:

$8^9 = 8 \times 8 \times 8 \times 8 \times 8 \times 8 \times 8 \times 8 \times 8$, where the number 8 appears nine times.

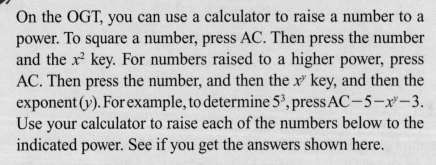

On the OGT, you can use a calculator to raise a number to a power. To square a number, press AC. Then press the number and the x^2 key. For numbers raised to a higher power, press AC. Then press the number, and then the x^y key, and then the exponent (y). For example, to determine 5^3, press AC $-5-x^y-3$. Use your calculator to raise each of the numbers below to the indicated power. See if you get the answers shown here.

15^2	=	225
16^1	=	16
8^4	=	4,096
20^2	=	400
9^5	=	59,049

Adding and Subtracting Powers

When adding or subtracting numbers raised to a power, put each number in standard form and then add or subtract the numbers. Remember that adding or subtracting numbers raised to powers does *not* involve adding or subtracting the powers, even if the bases are the same.

For example,

$$3^2 + 6^3 = 9 + 216 = 225$$
$$5^2 + 5^4 = 25 + 625 = 650$$
$$7^3 - 5^2 = 343 - 25 = 318$$

Multiplying and Dividing Powers

If the bases are different, put the numbers in standard form and multiply or divide:

$$3^4 \times 2^3 = 81 \times 8 = 648$$
$$7^3 \div 4^2 = 343 \div 16 \approx 21.44$$

When multiplying numbers with the same base, however, you keep the base the same and *add* only the exponents.

Therefore,

$$8^2 \times 8^3 = 8^{2+3} = 8^5$$
$$6^4 \times 6^{-2} = 6^{4-2} = 6^2$$

When dividing numbers with the same base, you keep the bases the same and *subtract* the exponents.

$$7^4 \div 7^2 = 7^{4-2} = 7^2$$
$$8^2 \div 8^4 = 8^{2-4} = 8^{-2}$$

Note that in the second example, the exponents are subtracted like this: $2 + (-4) = -2$.

If the bases are different, put the numbers in standard form and divide.

$$7^3 \div 4^2 = 343 \div 16 \approx 21.44$$

Let's Review 4: Ratios, Proportions, and Powers

Complete each of the following questions. Use the Tip below each question to help you choose the correct answer. When you finish, check your answers at the end of this chapter.

1. **A conservationist has been observing spider mites on spruce trees in her state. She recorded that 15 of the 75 spruce trees she observed throughout the state appeared to be infected with spider mites. The state has an estimated 200,000 spruce trees.**

   Based on her observations, approximately how many spruce trees would she predict are infected with spider mites?

   A. 15,000

   B. 20,000

   C. 40,000

   D. 100,000

TIP

You need to create a ratio to solve this problem. Begin with the ratio from the conservationist's sample, $\frac{15}{75}$, and then set up a proportion, letting x stand for the unknown value.

2. **The area of Ohio is about 4.5×10^4 square miles. The area of New Jersey is about 9.0×10^3 square miles. What is the difference between the area of Ohio and the area of New Jersey?**

   A. 13.5×10^3

   B. 3.6×10^7

   C. 3.6×10^2

   D. 3.6×10^4

TIP

To answer this question, you need to convert the square miles for each state into standard form. Then subtract the area of New Jersey from the area of Ohio and convert this number into scientific notation.

3. **Which expression is equivalent to $9^5/9^2$?**

   A. 1^3

   B. 9^2

   C. 9^3

   D. 9^7

TIP

Remember to subtract exponents when dividing numbers with the same base.

4. **For every $10 Rob spends in a discount store, he receives a coupon for $2 off his next purchase.**

   Determine how many coupons Rob will receive if he spends $140. Show your work. (2 points)

TIP

Read the question carefully. You're not looking for the monetary value of the coupon; you're trying to find how many coupons Rob will receive.

Computing Money Problems

Some questions on the OGT will involve adding, subtracting, multiplying, and dividing monetary amounts. These questions are about real-life situations. You might be asked to calculate the sale price of a discounted item, sales tax, or the interest on a short-term loan.

Discounts and Sale Prices

Some real-life questions will ask you to determine the amount of a discount for an item on sale or the sale price of an item. For example, you might be asked to determine a discount of 15% on shoes that cost $45.00. To do this with a paper and pencil, you would multiply 45 by .15 as shown here:

$$\begin{array}{r} 45 \\ \times .15 \\ \hline 225 \\ +450 \\ \hline 6.75 \end{array}$$

The discount is $6.75.

Other questions will ask you to determine the sale price of an item after a discount is applied. Read the problem below:

Megan wants to buy a mirror for her room that is usually priced at $85.00 and is now discounted by 40%. What is the sale price of the mirror?

To solve this problem using a pencil and paper, you would multiply .40 by 85 as shown here:

$$\begin{array}{r} 85 \\ \times .40 \\ \hline 00 \\ +3400 \\ \hline 34.00 \end{array}$$

Remember that $34 is the amount of the discount. This question asks you to find the sale price of the mirror, so you have to subtract $34 from $85:

$$\begin{array}{r} 85.00 \\ -34.00 \\ \hline 51.00 \end{array}$$

The sale price of the mirror is $51.00.

Sales Tax

You determine the sales tax on an item in much the same way that you determine a discount. Read this question:

Gail works in a small hardware store where the cash register does not compute the sales tax. If the sales tax is 7%, what amount should Gail add to a purchase of $10.00?

To answer this question, multiply 10 by 7%, or .07. The amount of sales tax Gail should add to a purchase of $10.00 is $0.70, or 70 cents.

Some questions might ask you to add the sales tax to the cost of item. Read this problem:

Brian wants to buy a bike that costs $125. He knows that he will have to pay 6% sales tax on the bike. How much money, including tax, does Brian need to buy the bike?

To answer this question, you have to calculate the sales tax and add it onto the cost of the bike. Multiply 125 by 6%, or .06. When you do this, you get $7.50. Now add this amount onto $125, the cost of the bike. The answer is $132.50. This is the amount of money Brian needs to buy the bike.

Interest

When you borrow money, you take a loan. Usually, you're asked to pay interest on the **principal**, the amount of money you borrowed. **Interest** is like a fee that you pay to the person or company that lent you the money. Interest is paid to the lender in addition to the principal. Calculating interest is usually very simple. Read this problem:

If Alberto borrows $5,000 from a bank at a fixed interest rate of 12% per year, how much interest must he pay if he pays the loan in full at the end of one year?

To solve this problem, you must multiply 5,000 by 12%, or .12. The answer is 600. If Alberto pays the loan in full at the end of one year, he must pay $600 in interest.

Let's Review 5: Computing Money Problems

Complete each of the following questions. Use the Tip below each question to help you choose the correct answer. When you finish, check your answers at the end of this chapter.

1. Mario wants to buy a skateboard that is regularly priced at $55 but is now discounted by 15%. What is the sale price of the skateboard?

    A. $8.25

    B. $46.75

    C. $56.75

    D. $82.50

 TIP Multiply 55 by .15 to find the discount. Then deduct this amount from the price of the skateboard.

2. Javier works in an ice cream store where the cash register does not compute the sales tax. Determine how much Javier should add to a purchase of $11.00 if the sales tax rate is 5%. Show your work. (2 points)

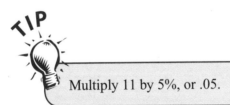 **TIP** Multiply 11 by 5%, or .05.

3. If a pair of jeans originally cost $25 and is selling at a 12% discount, what is the amount of this discount?

    A. $3.00

    B. $4.20

    C. $22.00

    D. $28.00

 TIP Multiply 25 by .12. This is the amount of the discount.

4. Leo's dental plan pays 45% of dental expenses after the deductible of $100 is subtracted. Leo's total dental bill was $380. What is the exact amount the dental plan will pay?

A. $109

B. $126

C. $226

D. $280

 TIP

Deduct 100 from 380 to find the expense after the deductible. Then find 45% of this number.

5. If Jason borrows $7,000 to buy a car at a fixed interest rate of 13% per year, how much interest must he pay if he pays the loan in full at the end of two years?

A. $910

B. $920

C. $1,820

D. $1,840

 TIP

Notice that this question asks you to determine the interest for two years. First find the interest for one year, and then multiply this number by two.

Chapter 2 Practice Problems

Complete each of the following practice problems. Check your answers at the end of this chapter. Be sure to read the answer explanations!

1. Which expression is equivalent to $9^2 \times 9^3$?

   A. 9^1

   B. 9^5

   C. 9^6

   D. 81^6

2. A party planner determines that for every 12 guests who attend the party, she will need 8 pounds of chicken. How many pounds of chicken will she need if 72 guests attend the party?

   A. 12

   B. 36

   C. 48

   D. 576

3. Kristen wants to buy a coat that is usually priced at $125 and is now discounted by 35%. What is the sale price of the coat?

   A. $43.75

   B. $81.25

   C. $90.00

   D. $91.50

4. Louis earns $15 per lawn to mow grass, and he mows 3 lawns per week. Determine how much Louis earns in 4 weeks. Show your work. (2 points)

5. Keisha's eyeglass plan pays 52% of the cost for a pair of glasses after the deductible of $25 is subtracted. Keisha's glasses cost $225. Which is the best estimate of the amount the insurance company will pay?

   A. $90

   B. $100

   C. $120

   D. $140

6. Which expression is equivalent to $5^6/5^2$?

   A. 1^4

   B. 5^4

   C. 5^8

   D. 5^{12}

7. If boots that originally cost $52 are selling at a 25% discount, what is the amount of the discount?

   A. $12

   B. $13

   C. $27

   D. $39

8. If Karen borrows $8,000 from a bank at a fixed interest rate of 14% per year, how much interest must she pay if she pays the loan in full at the end of one year?

A. $1,120

B. $2,120

C. $5,880

D. $6,880

9. Pedro wants to buy a birthday present for his mother that costs $32.00. He knows he must pay 7% sales tax on the gift. What amount should Pedro add to a purchase of $32.00?

A. $2.00

B. $2.24

C. $22.40

D. $29.76

10. Maurice would like to buy a bike that costs $132.50. The bike is on sale for 20% off, and 5% sales tax will be added onto the sale price of the bike. Approximately how much will Maurice have to pay for the bike?

A. $100.00

B. $110.00

C. $120.00

D. $130.00

Chapter 2 Answer Explanations

Let's Review 3: Estimation

1. C

The numbers should be rounded to the nearest ten: 30, 20, 70, and 10, and 99 should be rounded to 100. When you add these numbers, the answer is 230.

2. B

When you round $249.95 to $250.00, you can quickly determine that 10% of $250 is $25.

3. C

If you multiply 7×20, you get 140. If you multiply 140 by 10 (the number of weeks Sarah worked), the answer is $1,400.

4. B

If you round both numbers to the nearest ten thousand, you get 30,000 and 10,000. The difference between these numbers is 20,000.

Let's Review 4: Ratios, Proportions, and Powers

1. C

To solve this problem, reduce the fraction $\frac{15}{75}$ to $\frac{1}{5}$. Then set up a proportion like this:

$\frac{1}{5} = \frac{x}{200,000}$. Then cross-multiply:

$5x = 200,000$

Divide both sides by 5:

$$\frac{5x}{5} = \frac{200,000}{5}$$
$$x = 40,000$$

2. D

Begin by converting the square miles for each state into standard form:

$4.5 \times 10^4 = 45,000$

$9.0 \times 10^3 = 9,000$

Then subtract: $45,000 - 9,000 = 36,000 = 3.6 \times 10^4$.

3. C

You need to subtract the exponents and keep the base the same.

4. Sample answer:

For every $10 Rob spends, he gets a coupon, so the ratio of coupons to money spent is $\frac{1}{10}$.

$$\frac{1}{10} = \frac{x}{140}$$

Cross multiply to get:

$10x = 140$

$x = 14$ coupons

Note that the value of the coupon is not part of the solution because you are asked only to find how many coupons.

Let's Review 5: Computing Money Problems

1. B

When you multiply $55 by .15, you get $8.25. To find the sale price, subtract this amount from the original cost of the skateboard, and the answer is $46.75.

2. Sample answer:

To find the amount of the sales tax, you need to multiply $11 by .05. The answer is $0.55.

3. A

To solve this problem, you have to multiply $25 by .12. The amount of the discount is $3.00.

4. B

The first step in solving this problem is to subtract $100, the amount of Leo's deductible, from $380, the amount of his dental bill. Then multiply the answer, $280, by 45%, or .45, the portion paid by his dental plan. The answer is $126. This is the amount Leo's dental plan will pay.

5. C

To solve this problem you have to multiply $7,000 by .13. The answer is $910. However, since you need to find the amount of interest Javier would pay in two years, you need to multiply $910 by 2.

Chapter 2 Practice Problems

1. B

When multiplying numbers with the same base, add the exponents and keep the base the same.

2. C

You have to set up a proportion to solve this problem:

$$\frac{8}{12} = \frac{x}{72}, \text{ or}$$
$$\frac{2}{3} = \frac{x}{72}$$

Cross multiply to get:

$$3x = 144$$

Divide both sides by 3:

$$\frac{3x}{3} = \frac{144}{3}$$

$$x = 48$$

3. B

To solve this problem, multiply 125 by .35 to find the discount. Then deduct this amount from the original price of the coat.

4. Sample answer:

Each week Louis earns $3 \times \$15 = \$45$. In four weeks, he will earn $4 \times \$45 = \$180$.

5. B

If you deduct $25 from $225, you get $200. If you multiply $200 by .52, the answer is $104. The best estimate is B, $100.

6. B

When dividing numbers with the same base, subtract the exponents.

7. B

If you multiply the price of the boots, $52 by .25, the amount of the discount, the answer is $13.

8. A

To solve this problem you have to multiply $8,000, the amount of money Karen borrowed, by .14, the rate of the interest. The answer is $1,120.

9. B

To find the sales tax on $32, multiply this number by .07, the rate of the sales tax. The answer is $2.24. This is the amount that Pedro should add to the cost of the purchase.

10. B

You can estimate this answer by rounding $132.50 to $130 and multiplying this number by 20% to determine the discount. Subtract the discount from the original price to find the sale price, and add 5% of this number for the total price.

$130 × .20 = $26

$130 − $26 = $104 = price of bike after the discount is applied.

$104 × .05 = $5.20 = sales tax on discounted bike price.

$104 + $5.20 - $109.20 ≈ $110.

Chapter 3
Data Analysis and Probability, Part 1

Benchmarks

C. Compare the characteristics of the mean, median, and mode for a given set of data, and explain which measure of center best represents the data.

D. Find, use, and interpret measures of center and spread, such as mean and quartiles, and use those measures to compare and draw conclusions about sets of data.

H. Use counting techniques, such as permutations and combinations, to determine the total number of options and possible outcomes.

I. Design an experiment to test a theoretical probability, and record and explain results.

J. Compute probabilities of compound events, independent events, and simple dependent events.

K. Make predictions based on theoretical probabilities and experimental results.

In this chapter, you will learn how to solve data analysis problems involving probability and measures of central tendency. **Probability** refers to the odds that an event will happen. Like many questions on the OGT, probability problems often involve real-life situations.

The **measures of central tendency** include mean, mode, median. In this chapter, you will learn how to determine each of these for a set of data as well as the range, and you will learn how to tell which yields the highest or lowest result for a given set of data.

Probability

Probability can be determined by using this formula:

P = number of favorable outcomes/number of possible outcomes

Probability can be expressed as a fraction, a decimal, a percent, or a ratio. Most of the time on the OGT, probability is expressed as a fraction or a percent.

Read this problem:

Find the probability of spinning a "3" on the spinner below.

A. 0

B. $\frac{1}{4}$

C. $\frac{1}{2}$

D. 1

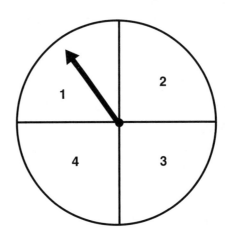

To solve this problem, use the formula for probability with the following values:

1 = number of favorable outcomes
4 = number of possible outcomes

By using this formula, you can see that the probability of spinning a 3 on the spinner is $\frac{1}{4}$. Answer choice B is correct. Let's try another problem:

Justine has a bag of 20 marbles. Ten of these marbles are white, 3 are green, 2 are blue, and 5 are yellow. If Justine reaches into the bag and pulls out a marble without looking, what is the probability that she will pull out a yellow marble?

A. 0

B. 5%

C. 25%

D. 50%

Use the probability formula to solve this problem. There are 5 yellow marbles, so this is the number of favorable outcomes. There are 20 marbles altogether, so this is the number of possible outcomes. The probability that Justine will pull out a yellow marble is $\frac{5}{20}$. If you convert this fraction to a decimal, it is .25. Then if you convert the decimal to a percent, it is 25%. Answer choice C is correct.

Let's try another problem:

There are 10 straws in a box; some are white and some are red. The probability of reaching into the box and selecting a white straw is $\frac{2}{5}$. How many red straws are in the box?

A. 1

B. 6

C. 8

D. 10

You know that the probability of reaching into the box and pulling out a white straw is $\frac{2}{5}$. Therefore, $\frac{2}{5}$ of the 10 straws are white:

$$\frac{2}{5} \times 10 = 4$$

Four straws are white, so the rest $(10 - 4 = 6)$ must be red.

So the number of red straws in the box is 6, and answer choice B is correct.

Let's Review 6: Probability

Complete each of the following questions. Use the Tip below each question to help you choose the correct answer. When you finish, check your answers at the end of this chapter.

1. **Find the probability of spinning "green" on the spinner below.**

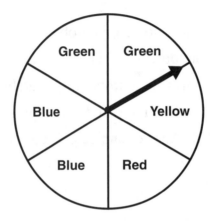

A. 0

B. $\dfrac{1}{4}$

C. $\dfrac{1}{3}$

D. $\dfrac{1}{2}$

TIP

Remember to use the formula for probability and then reduce the fraction. There are six sections on the spinner, and two of these sections are green.

2. A bag contains 8 white chips, 5 red chips, 3 black chips, 2 blue chips, and 2 green chips. If you reach into the bag without looking, what is the probability that you will pull out a red chip?

A. 25%

B. 33%

C. 67%

D. 55%

> **TIP**
> There are 20 chips altogether and 5 of these chips are red.

3. Peter is going to roll a six-sided number cube. What is the probability of rolling an even number?

A. $\frac{1}{6}$

B. $\frac{1}{4}$

C. $\frac{1}{3}$

> **TIP**
> A six-sided number cube has sides numbered 1, 2, 3, 4, 5, and 6.

D. $\frac{1}{2}$

4. There are eight jelly beans in a jar; some are pink and some are yellow. The probability of randomly reaching into the jar and selecting a pink jelly bean is $\frac{1}{4}$. What is the probability of pulling out a yellow jelly bean?

A. 25%

B. 50%

C. 60%

> **TIP**
> The probability of picking a pink jelly bean is $\frac{1}{4}$, or 25%. All the rest are yellow.

D. 75%

5. **If a penny is tossed ten times, and on the first five tosses it comes up heads, what is the probability of getting heads on the sixth toss?**

A. $\dfrac{1}{4}$

B. $\dfrac{1}{3}$

C. $\dfrac{1}{2}$

D. 1

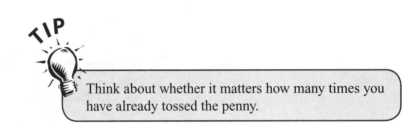

TIP

Think about whether it matters how many times you have already tossed the penny.

Combinations

Questions about combinations might be, for example, to determine how many combinations of ice-cream flavor and cone are available at an ice-cream stand. Drawing a tree diagram can help you answer these questions. For example, look at this problem:

For her school uniform, Susan has a choice between a tan blazer and a blue blazer. She can wear tan, blue, or black pants. How many combinations of blazer and pants does Susan have?

Creating a tree diagram like the one shown here can help you answer this question. Each line shows one of the possible combinations.

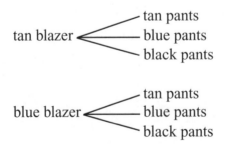

tan blazer
— tan pants
— blue pants
— black pants

blue blazer
— tan pants
— blue pants
— black pants

Now, count the lines. Susan has six combinations of blazer and pants.

Let's Review 7: Combinations

Complete each of the following questions. Use the Tip below each question to help you choose the correct answer. When you finish, check your answers at the end of this chapter.

1. **Customers at a pizza shop have a choice of thin crust, wheat crust, or thick crust and a choice of extra cheese, olives, pepperoni, sausage, or mushrooms as toppings. How many combinations of crust and one topping are there?**

A. 8

B. 10

C. 15

D. 30

TIP

Make a diagram and draw lines from each kind of crust to each topping.

2. **Sandy bought six books. She plans to read two of these while on vacation. How many combinations of two books from the group of six could she choose to read?**

A. 10

B. 15

C. 20

D. 30

TIP

Making a tree diagram will help you to answer this question. Note that picking books 1 and 2 is the same as picking books 2 and 1, so don't count duplicate pairings.

Mean, Median, Mode, and Range

You can analyze data by finding measures of central tendency, including the mean, median, and mode, and the range of the data. **Mean** is another word for "average." To find the mean of a set of numbers, add all of the numbers together and divide by the number of items that make up that total. Look at this set of numbers:

$$2, 4, 6, 8, 10$$

To find the mean, you first add all of the numbers:

$$2 + 4 + 6 + 8 + 10 = 30$$

Then you divide 30 by the number of items, in this case 5. The mean of these numbers is therefore 6.

The **median** of a set of numbers is the middle number when the numbers are arranged by size. It's not the average, but simply the number in the middle. Look at this set of numbers:

$$12, 8, 20, 4, 6$$

To find the median, you need to put them in order from least to greatest (or greatest to least):

$$4, 6, 8, 12, 20$$

When the numbers are in order from least to greatest, you can see that the number 8 is the median. When you have an even number of scores, after they are listed from smallest to largest, add the two middle scores together and divide by two. That will be the median score.

The **mode** of a set of data is the most frequently occurring number. Look at the numbers below:

$$88, 92, 76, 42, 88, 90, 100, 110, 115$$

The mode of these numbers is 88, the only number that occurs more than once.

The **range** of a set of data is the difference between the smallest number and the greatest number. Consider these numbers again:

$$88, 92, 76, 42, 88, 90, 100, 110, 115$$

The smallest number is 42 and the greatest is 115. To find the range, subtract 42 from 115:

$$115 - 42 = 73$$

The range of this set of numbers is 73.

Now read this problem, the kind of problem about central tendency that you might see on the OGT:

The scores on Mr. Seymour's English test were 98, 60, 88, 87, 96, 79, 80, 58, 76, 99, 80, 58, 76, 99, 90, 87, 62, 76, 89, and 97. What is the range of these scores?

To determine the range of this problem, subtract the lowest test score, 58, from the highest test score, 99.

$$99 - 58 = 41$$

Forty-one is the correct answer. Now let's try this problem:

If the mean number of people who attended an amusement park over 5 days is 25,000, what was the total attendance during the 5 days?

A. 5,000

B. 50,000

C. 125,000

D. 250,000

To solve this problem, you need to multiply the number of days by the mean. In this case, you would multiply 5 × 25,000. The answer is C, 125,000.

Let's Review 8: Mean, Median, Mode, and Range

Complete each of the following questions. Use the Tip below each question to help you choose the correct answer. When you finish, check your answers at the end of this chapter.

1. The office manager in a small office is considering hiring a receptionist to answer the telephone. To see whether a receptionist is needed, the employees used a log to record the number of calls answered each day. The data recorded in a 14-day period are shown below.

    10, 12, 8, 16, 6, 5, 8, 5, 12, 13, 12, 12, 8, 6

    Which measure of central tendency reflects the greatest number of calls during the 14-day period?

    A. mean

    B. mode

    C. median

    D. range

 TIP Calculate the measure in each answer choice. Then choose the highest number.

2. The number of cars sold at Ray's Used Automobiles was 12 in January, 22 in February, 30 in March, 42 in April, and 58 in May. What is the range in the number of cars sold from January to May?

    A. 12

    B. 33

    C. 46

    D. 70

 TIP Remember that the range is the difference between the smallest and largest numbers.

3. The total points scored for the Warriors basketball team for each game during the season were 42, 20, 13, 64, 27, 35, 45, 40, 23, 12, 12, and 39. What is their mean score?

A. 12

B. 31

C. 35

D. 372

TIP

To find the mean of this data, add the numbers, and then divide by the total number of items.

4. The number of tickets sold by each grade at Central Elementary are shown in the table below.

Grade	Number of Tickets Sold
1	246
2	112
3	493
4	98
5	209
6	112
7	190

Use the data in the table to determine the median.

A. 98

B. 112

C. 190

D. 209

TIP

Put the number of tickets sold in order from least to greatest. The median is the number in the middle.

5. Renee's grades in World Cultures were 84, 85, 95, 88, 92, 100, 82, and 78. What is her mean grade? (2 points)

TIP

To find the mean, add together all of her grades, and then divide by the number of grades.

Chapter 3 Practice Problems

Complete each of the following practice problems. Check your answers at the end of this chapter. Be sure to read the answer explanations!

1. There are 12 coins in a box; some are nickels and some are pennies. The probability of randomly reaching into the box and pulling out a nickel is $\frac{2}{3}$. What is the probability of pulling out a penny?

A. $\frac{1}{8}$

B. $\frac{1}{4}$

C. $\frac{1}{3}$

D. $\frac{2}{3}$

2. Students at Central High School will begin wearing uniforms in the fall. Each student will have three differently colored shirts (blue, white, and striped) and two differently colored pairs of pants (tan or navy). A student's uniform consists of one shirt, and one pair of pants.

    Determine the total number of different uniforms a student can wear. (2 points)

3. The weekly salaries of seven employees are $160, $240, $260, $85, $200, $180, and $120. What is the median salary?

    A. $120

    B. $160

    C. $180

    D. $200

4. Find the probability of spinning 4 on the spinner below.

    A. 13%

    B. 25%

    C. 33%

    D. 50%

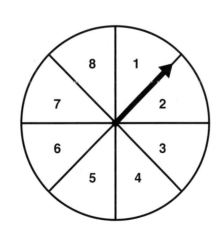

5. **The average monthly high temperature in Sarasota, Florida, is shown in the table below.**

Month	Average High Temperature
January	72°
February	74°
March	78°
April	82°
May	87°
June	90°
July	91°
August	91°
September	90°
October	85°
November	79°
December	74°

Use the chart to determine the range.

A. 19°

B. 20°

C. 83°

D. 91°

6. Christine has a bag of 25 marbles. Five of these marbles are green, 4 are blue, 3 are white, 8 are black, and 5 are yellow. If Christine reaches into the bag, what is the probability that she will randomly pull out a yellow marble?

A. $\dfrac{1}{8}$

B. $\dfrac{1}{5}$

C. $\dfrac{1}{4}$

D. $\dfrac{1}{3}$

7. At a pizza shop, six different toppings are available: sausage, mushrooms, pepperoni, green peppers, anchovies, and olives.

    A customer wants to order a pizza with two different toppings.

    Using the six toppings listed, determine the total number of different possibilities for a pizza with two different toppings. (4 points)

8. Kayla recorded the hours she spent studying each week for five weeks. She listed these hours in the chart below.

Week	Hours Spent Studying
1	18
2	12
3	15
4	5
5	10

What is the mean number of hours Kayla spent studying?

A. 10

B. 12

C. 13

D. 15

9. The miles Michelle ran each day in a given week are as follows: 2, 3, 3, 4, 4, 3, and 6. What is the mode of the number of miles Michelle ran?

A. 3

B. 4

C. 5

D. 6

Chapter 3 Answer Explanations

Let's Review 6: Probability

1. C

The spinner is divided into six sections and two of these sections are green. So the probability that the spinner will land on green is $\frac{2}{6}$ or $\frac{1}{3}$.

2. A

The bag contains 20 chips altogether, and 5 of these chips are red. The probability of pulling out a red chip is $\frac{5}{20}$ or $\frac{1}{4}$. This fraction is equivalent to 25%.

3. D

If the number cube has six sides numbered 1, 2, 3, 4, 5, and 6, three of the six sides are even. Therefore, the probability of rolling an even number is $\frac{3}{6}$, or $\frac{1}{2}$.

4. D

The probability of picking a pink jelly bean is 25%. The rest, or the remaining 75%, must be yellow.

5. C

If you toss a penny, the odds of it coming up heads is $\frac{1}{2}$. The odds are always $\frac{1}{2}$ regardless of how many times you toss the penny.

Let's Review 7: Combinations

1. C

If you write down the kinds of crusts: thin, wheat, and thick, and then jot down the toppings and draw a line from each kind of crust to each topping, you'll see that there are 15 combinations.

2. B

To solve this problem, write the numbers 1 through 6 in a line. Then draw a line from 1 to 2, 1 to 3, 1 to 4, and so on. There are 5 pairings. Do the same for book 2, but remember that you wouldn't pair 2 to 1 again because you already have the pairing 1 to 2, and it's the same thing. There are 4 pairings for book 2. Continue for each remaining book, making sure you don't duplicate pairs. The number of pairings will be 5 + 4 + 3 + 2 + 1 + 0 = 15.

Let's Review 8: Mean, Median, Mode, and Range

1. B

To solve this problem, you need to calculate each measure and choose the measure showing the greatest number of calls. The mean is 9.5, the mode is 12, the median is 9 (the average of 8 and 10), and the range is 11. Therefore, the mode shows the greatest number of calls.

2. C

To find the range in the number of cars sold from January to May, subtract the smallest number, 12, from the greatest number, 58. The range is 46.

3. B

When you add all of the numbers, you get 372. When you divide 372 by the number of items, 12, you get 31, the correct answer.

4. C

If you put the numbers in order from least to greatest, you'll see that 190 is in the middle. This number is the median.

5. 88

If you add together all of Renee's grades, the total is 704. When you divide this number by 8, the number of grades, you get 88, the mean.

Chapter 3 Practice Problems

1. C

Of the 12 coins, $\frac{2}{3}$ are nickels, or $12 \times \frac{2}{3} = 8$ nickels. So 4 are pennies, and the probability of pulling out a penny is thus $\frac{4}{12} = \frac{1}{3}$.

2. 6

The combinations of shirts and pants can be listed like this: BB, BT, WB, WT, SB, ST. There are six combinations.

3. C

If you put the salaries in order from least to greatest, you'll see that $180 is the median (middle) salary.

4. A

The spinner has eight sections and only one section is numbered "4," so the probability of spinning a 4 is $\frac{1}{8}$, which equals approximately .13, or 13%.

5. A

To find the range of the average monthly temperatures, subtract the lowest temperature, 72°F, from the highest temperature, 91°F.

6. B

There are 25 marbles in the bag and 5 of them are yellow. Therefore, the probability of choosing a yellow marble is $\frac{5}{25}$, or $\frac{1}{5}$.

7. 15

If you pair up each of the toppings, you'll see that there are 15 different combinations of two toppings. Remember that a pizza with sausage and mushrooms is the same as a pizza with mushrooms and sausage.

8. B

When you add all of the hours Kayla spent studying, you get 60. When you divide 60 by 5, the answer is 12.

9. A

The mode is the most frequently occurring number. In this case, it is the number 3.

Chapter 4

Data Analysis and Probability, Part 2

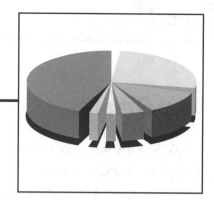

Benchmarks

A. Create, interpret, and use graphical displays and statistical measures to describe data; e.g., box-and-whiskers plots, histograms, scatterplots, measures of center and variability.

B. Evaluate different graphical representations of the same data to determine which is the most appropriate representation for an identified purpose.

E. Evaluate the validity of claims and predictions that are based on data by examining the appropriateness of the data collection and analysis.

F. Construct convincing arguments based on analysis of data and interpretation of graphs.

G. Describe sampling methods and analyze the effects of method chosen on how well the resulting sample represents the population.

In the previous chapter, you learned how to analyze a set of data to determine probability and measures of central tendency. In this chapter, you'll learn how to analyze data displayed in different forms. Some questions on the OGT will be about data displayed in line, bar, and circle graphs. You need to be able to interpret data in these graphs to answer these questions. Other questions will be about data displayed in plots such as scatter plots, box-and-whisker plots, and stem-and-leaf plots. You'll learn these graphs and plots in this chapter.

Line Graphs

A **line graph** is a very popular type of graph that compares two variables—one along the *x*-axis and one along the *y*-axis. Unlike in a bar graph, the two variables being compared in a line graph are closely related; a change in one variable is associated with a change in the second variable. A line graph is a great way to show trends. Look at this line graph:

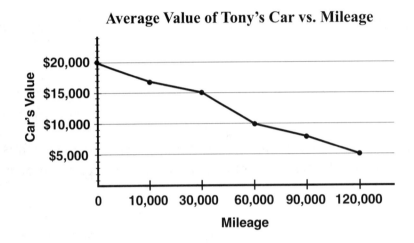

You can see from this line graph that as the number of miles on Tony's car increases, the value of the car decreases.

Bar Graphs

In a **bar graph**, the height or length of a bar shows the number of something. The higher or longer the bar, the greater the value. A bar graph has a *x*- and a *y*-axis. It is a good way to show comparisons and can show trends, such as changes in sales over time.

While a bar graph can have either vertical or horizontal bars, most bar graphs on the OGT have vertical bars. Look at this bar graph. It shows the number of cars manufactured at a factory over five years.

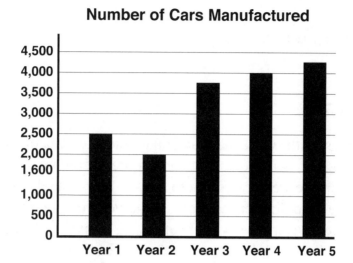

In this bar graph, Years 1 through 5 are listed on the x-axis and the number of cars manufactured is listed on the *y*-axis. You can tell, by just glancing at the graph, that the greatest number of cars were manufactured in Year 5 and that, except for Year 2, the number of cars manufactured increased each year.

Circle Graphs

A **circle graph**, also called a **pie chart** or **pie graph**, is often used to display the division of a whole or parts of a whole. Data in a circle graph is often displayed in percentages. Circle graphs work best to show large divisions, such as the division of money in a household budget. Look at this circle graph:

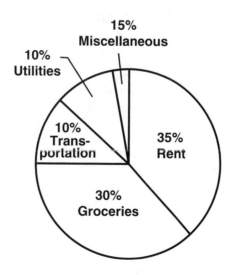

Miller Family Monthly Budget

You can see from this circle graph that the Miller family spends most of its monthly income on rent and groceries.

Venn Diagrams

Some questions on the OGT may ask you to interpret data displayed in a Venn diagram. A **Venn diagram** is made up of two or more overlapping circles and is used to display relationships between two or more sets of data. Venn diagrams are a great way to show similarities and differences. Look at the Venn diagram below. If this diagram were filled in, it would compare two sets of a data, A and B. The part of the circle that overlaps, C, would list ways that the sets of data are alike. Traits unique to each set of data would be in the part of the circles that do not overlap.

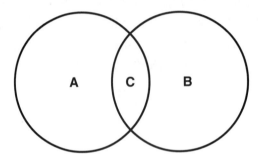

A Venn diagram comparing three sets of data would look like the one shown here. Note that the ways in which A and B are alike would be listed where circle A and circle B overlap. The ways in which A and C are alike would be listed where circles A and C overlap, and the ways in which B and C are alike would be listed where circles B and C overlap. The ways in which A, B, and C are alike would be listed in the small area where all three circles overlap.

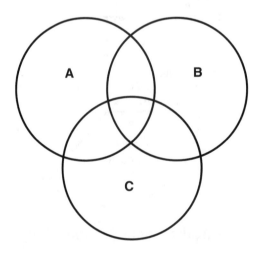

Let's Review 9: Graphs

Complete each of the following questions. Use the Tip below each question to help you choose the correct answer. When you finish, check your answers at the end of this chapter.

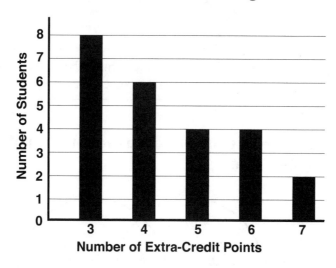

Extra-Credit Points in English

1. **The distribution of extra-credit points in Ms. Washington's English class is shown on the graph above. How many more students received five extra-credit points than seven extra-credit points?**

A. 2

B. 3

C. 4

D. 5

TIP

To answer this question, look at the bar for five extra-credit points and the bar for seven extra-credit points. Subtract the number of students receiving five extra-credit points from the number of students receiving seven.

2. Alanis surveyed the students in her school to see what they like to do in their spare time. About 45% of the students said they like to listen to music, 20% like to play sports, 22% like to read, and 13% like to do something else.

    Which type of graph is appropriate to display the data Alanis collected in her survey?

    A. line graph

    B. bar graph

    C. circle graph

    D. Venn diagram

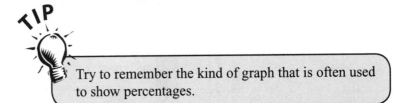

TIP
Try to remember the kind of graph that is often used to show percentages.

3. Bethany constructed a diagram to illustrate the number of students in her class that have a pet.

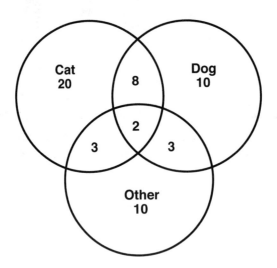

    How many more students have a cat than a dog?

    A. 8

    B. 10

    C. 20

    D. 30

TIP
To answer this question, subtract the number of students with a dog from the number of students with a cat.

4. How many students have both a dog, a cat, and another type of pet?

A. 2

B. 3

C. 8

D. 40

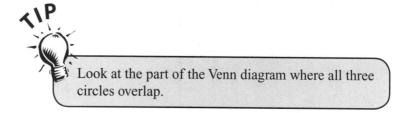

TIP

Look at the part of the Venn diagram where all three circles overlap.

Scatter Plots

A **scatter plot** shows at a glance whether there is a relationship between two sets of data. In a scatter plot, data is plotted using dots. If the dots show a trend, a line is drawn. If the line is increasing from left to right, the trend is said to be positive. Look at the scatter plot shown here. It shows whether students who play a musical instrument tend to get higher grades in school.

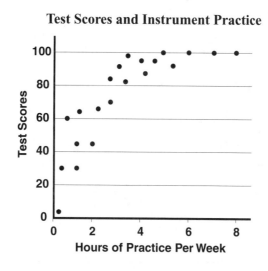

According to the scatter plot above, students who play a musical instrument tend to earn higher grades. In fact, the more hours per week they practice playing an instrument, the higher their grades are.

Now look at this scatter plot. It compares the same two variables, but this time it shows a negative trend.

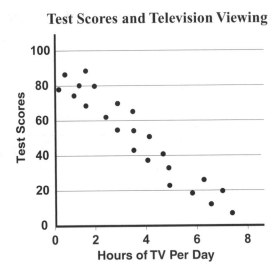

This scatter plot shows that students who spend more time watching televison get lower grades.

Sometimes a scatter plot will show no trend between two variables. The scatter plot below shows no trend between time spent sleeping and getting good grades.

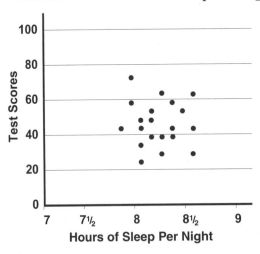

Box-and-Whisker Plots

On the OGT, you might be asked to interpret data displayed in a box-and-whisker plot. A **box-and-whisker plot** is a great way to display large quantities of data. This type of plot looks like a box with two lines extending from it placed over a number line. In this type of plot, the lowest number in a set of data is shown by the leftmost horizontal line extending from the box, and the greatest number in a set of data is shown by the rightmost horizontal line. The median of the entire set of data is plotted with the horizontal line in the center of the box. This is called the **second quartile**. Then the median of the data in between this median and the leftmost extreme is found. This is called the first quartile and is shown by the left end of the box. In other words, the first quartile is the median of the lower part of the data. Then the median of the data in between this median and the rightmost extreme is found. This is called the **third quartile** and is shown by the right end of the box. The third quartile is the median of the upper part of the data. Look at the box-and-whiskers plot below and study each of its parts.

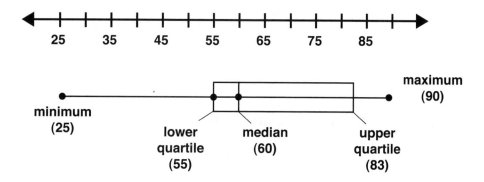

Stem-and-Leaf Plots

In a **stem-and-leaf plot**, each number in a set of data is split into a stem and a leaf. The first number goes into the stem column and the second goes into the leaf column. This type of plot makes it easy to categorize data and see a trend.

Imagine that a teacher wanted to create a stem-and-leaf plot to show these test scores: 99, 92, 86, 85, 74, 68, 71, 70, 85, 82, 83, 95, 80, 90. It would look like this:

Stem	Leaf
6	8
7	0 1 4
8	0 2 3 5 5 6
9	0 2 5 9

The tens numeral becomes the stem. The units numerals become the leaves. For 68, 6 is the stem and 8 is a leaf. By creating a stem-and-leaf plot, the teacher would be able to see the distribution of test scores.

Bias

You might be asked a question on the OGT in which you would have to choose the best sampling method. The trick here is to stay away from an answer choice that would make the sample biased, or unfair, because the people sampled are likely to feel a certain way. Read this question:

Javier wants to conduct a survey to see how many students are interested in joining a new school club.

Which sample population should Javier survey to represent the entire student body?

A. survey the teachers

B. survey the captain from each sports team

C. randomly survey two people from each homeroom class

D. randomly survey 50 people from the freshman class

To answer this question correctly, you need to choose the sample that is most fair. You can eliminate answer choice A, because surveying the teachers wouldn't give Javier an idea of how many students are interested in joining a new club. Answer choice B might be biased, since the captains of sports teams might enjoy the same activities. Answer choice C is a good answer, especially since Javier is randomly choosing two students per class. Answer choice D is also biased, because students in the freshman class are all the same age and might not be a good representation of the whole school. Answer C is the best answer because it gives a sample from the entire school.

Let's Review 10: Plots

Complete each of the following questions. Use the Tip below each question to help you choose the correct answer. When you finish, check your answers at the end of this chapter.

1. **The box-and-whisker plot shows the number of points Tyler's basketball team scored per game during the basketball season.**

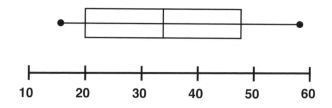

    Which statement can be made about the data, using the graph alone?

A. Tyler's basketball team's median score per game was 32.

B. Tyler's basketball team's median score per game was 42.

C. Tyler's basketball team's highest score per game was 32.

D. Tyler's basketball team's highest score during the season was 42.

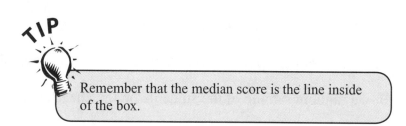

Remember that the median score is the line inside of the box.

2. The following stem-and-leaf plot shows the hourly wages of 20 workers. The workers are performing similar tasks but, because of differences in length of work experience and skill, are paid at different rates.

Stem	Leaf
10	5 6 7 7
11	3 4 4 6 6 9
12	0 0 5 5 7
13	0 0 0 1 3

Key
10	5 = $10.50

Determine the percentage of workers who are paid less than $12 per hour. (2 points)

Count the number of workers who are paid less than $12 an hour. This number should be the numerator and the denominator is 20, the total number of workers. Divide 20 into 12 to get a decimal. Then convert to a percentage.

3. Karen wants to determine the favorite musical band of the students in her high school.

Which sample should she use?

A. a random sample of the students in the environmental club

B. a random sample of the students on the cheerleading squad

C. a random sample of the students in the library during fifth period

D. a random sample of students on the official school roster

Choose the sample that would not be biased in any way.

Chapter 4 Practice Problems

Complete each of the following practice problems. Check your answers at the end of this chapter. Be sure to read the answer explanations!

1. **Mr. Sassy constructed a diagram to illustrate the number of seniors enrolled in honors courses.**

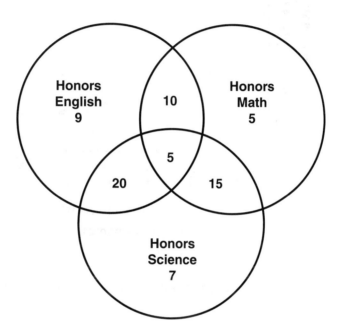

    How many seniors are enrolled in Honors Math?

A. 15

B. 20

C. 35

D. 45

2. **The scatter plot below shows high and low temperature information for Dallas, Texas, for six consecutive months.**

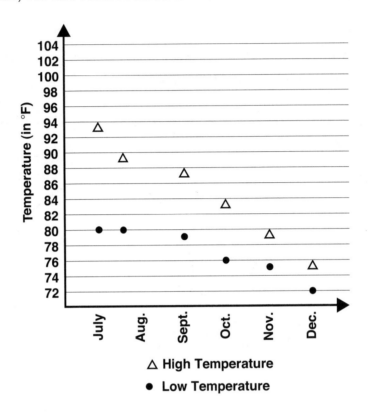

△ **High Temperature**
● **Low Temperature**

Determine the mean high temperature. Show or explain how you made your determination.

Draw a conclusion from the information plotted in the scatter plot.

A friend would like to vacation in Dallas, but she doesn't like very high temperatures. During what month would you suggest that your friend go on her vacation? Explain your answer.

3. The box-and-whisker plot below shows the number of points that the students in Ms. Garcia's class scored on a test.

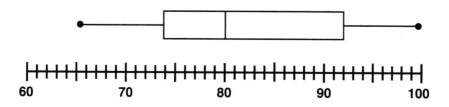

    Which statement can be made about the data, using the graph above?

A. The mean score on the test was 92.

B. The mean score on the test was 100.

C. The highest score on the test was 92.

D. The highest score on the test was 100.

4. The ages of the residents on the third floor in West Side Retirement Home are plotted on the stem-and-leaf plot below.

Stem	Leaf
6	0, 0, 3, 4, 5, 7, 8
7	0, 1, 4, 7, 9
8	0, 2, 3, 4, 6
9	0, 0, 0, 1, 2

Key
6	0 = 60 years

Key 6 (horizontal line) = 60 years

Determine the percentage of residents who are 80 years old or older. (2 points)

5.

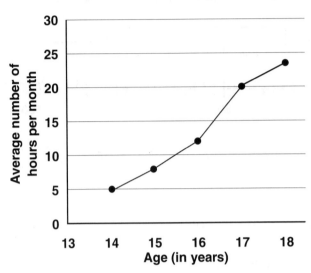

Number of Hours of Community Service

How many hours per month on average did the seventeen-year-olds work?

A. 8

B. 12

C. 20

D. 24

6. How many more hours did the eighteen-year-olds work than the fourteen-year-olds?

A. 5 hours

B. 19 hours

C. 24 hours

D. 29 hours

7. The results of a poll asking, "What kind of music is your favorite?" are shown in the circle graph below.

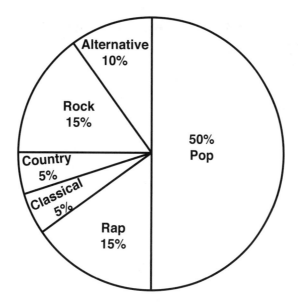

What percentage of people selected either alternative, pop, or classical as their favorite kind of music?

A. 25%

B. 60%

C. 65%

D. 75%

8. Cindy wants to conduct a survey to see how many people in her town would like a new park.

Which sample population should Cindy survey to represent the entire town?

A. survey town officials

B. survey people in the library on a Saturday

C. randomly survey kids in her school

D. randomly survey 50 people downtown

9. **For a research report, Chris recorded the population of his town over the last five years.**

   Which kind of data display would be an appropriate way to display Chris's research?

   A. line graph

   B. circle graph

   C. Venn diagram

   D. stem-and-leaf plot

Chapter 4 Answer Explanations

Let's Review 9: Graphs

1. A

Four students received five extra-credit points and two students received seven extra-credit points. If you subtract these two numbers, the answer is 2.

2. C

A circle graph is the best way to display percentages.

3. B

To correctly answer this question, you have to subtract the number of students with a dog as a pet from the number of students with a cat for a pet. Students who own both a dog and a cat are included in each count. $33 - 23 = 10$.

4. A

The number in the part where all three circles overlap is two.

Let's Review 10: Plots

1. A

The median score is the vertical line inside the box. In this case, it's 32.

2. 50%

To answer this question, put the number of workers earning less than $12, which is 10, over the total number of workers, 20, and convert to a percentage. The fraction is 10/20, which is equal to 50%.

3. D

Answer choice A might be biased, since students in the environmental club may share similar interests that are not representative of the whole school population; the same is true for answer choice B. Answer choice C might be biased because students from one particular class might be in the library during fifth period. Answer choice D is the best answer.

Chapter 4 Practice Problems

1. C

This information can be found in the second circle: $10 + 15 + 5 + 5 = 35$ seniors are enrolled in Honors Math.

2. Sample answer:

To determine the mean high temperature, add the high temperatures: 94, 90, 88, 84, 80 and 76. The mean of these temperatures is about 85. You can conclude that both the high and low temperatures drop steadily from July through to December. If your friend doesn't like high temperatures, she should plan her vacation to Dallas during the month of December, when it is the coolest.

3. D

The only conclusion supported by the plot is that the highest score was 100.

4. 45%

To determine the answer to this question, count the number of residents who are 80 or older. There are 10. The total number of residents is 22. If you change $\frac{10}{22}$ to an equivalent percentage, the answer is 45%.

5. C

To find the answer to this question, you have to look at the value for the average number of hours for 17-year-olds. It is 20.

6. B

The 18-year-olds worked 24 hours and the 14-year-olds worked 5 hours. If you subtract 5 from 24, the answer is 19.

7. C

If you add the percentages for pop (50%), alternative (10%) and classical (5%), the answer is 65%.

8. D

Answer choice D is the best answer because it is least likely to be biased.

9. A

A line graph is a good way to display trends in data over time.

Chapter 5

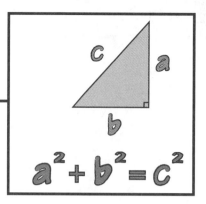

Geometry and Spatial Sense, Part 1

Benchmarks

A. Formally define geometric figures.

B. Describe and apply the properties of similar and congruent figures; and justify conjectures involving similarity and congruence.

C. Recognize and apply angle relationships in situations involving intersecting lines, perpendicular lines, and parallel lines.

I. Use right triangle trigonometric relationships to determine lengths and angle measures.

In this chapter, you'll learn some properties for plane (two-dimensional, or "flat") figures and three-dimensional figures. It's important to learn the properties of the figures discussed in this chapter because they are involved in many problems on the OGT. You'll also learn about lines and angles in this chapter and you'll learn how to use the Pythagorean Theorem to find the lengths of sides in right triangles.

Congruent Figures

Figures that are **congruent** are exactly the same size and shape. If you place two congruent figures on top of each other, they will fit exactly. The rectangles that follow are congruent. The sign indicating that figures are congruent is ≅.

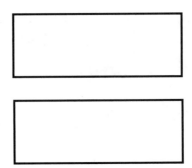

These triangles are also congruent:

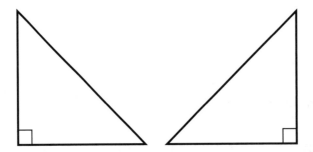

Plane Figures

A **plane figure** is a flat, closed figure. The chart below lists some common plane figures.

PLANE FIGURES

Figure	Description	Example
Rectangle	Has four right angles and four sides; sides across from each other are parallel and equal in length. The sum of the angles in a rectangle is 360°.	
Square	Has four right angles and four sides equal in length. The sum of the angles in a square is 360°.	

(continued on next page)

PLANE FIGURES (continued)

Rhombus	Has four equal sides, but may or may not have right angles. The sum of the angles in a rhombus is 360°.	
Parallelogram	Has four sides and two pair of opposite, parallel sides. The sum of the angles in a parallelogram is 360°.	
Trapezoid	Has four sides and one pair of parallel sides; it may or may not have a right angle. The sum of the angles in a trapezoid is 360°.	
Triangle	Has three sides; the lengths of the sides can vary. The sum of the angles in a triangle is 180°.	
Circle	Has no "sides." The sum of the degrees in a circle is 360°. All points are the same distance from the center.	
Pentagon	Has five sides that may or may not be equal. The sum of the angles in a pentagon is 540°. In a regular pentagon, all sides are equal and each angle measures 108°.	
Hexagon	Has six sides that may or may not be equal. The sum of the angles in a hexagon is 720°. In a regular hexagon, all side are equal and each angle is 120°.	

(continued on next page)

PLANE FIGURES (continued)

Octagon	Has eight sides that may or not be equal. The sum of the angles in an octagon is 1,080°. In a regular octagon, all sides are equal and each angle measures 135°.	
Polygon	Any two-dimensional shape whose sides are all straight lines. All of the figures in this table (except the circle) are polygons.	

Three-Dimensional Figures

Three-dimensional figures are different from plane figures because they are not flat—they also have width. Notice that there are special names for parts of three-dimensional shapes. Each flat part on a three-dimensional shape is called a **face**. The flat parts are actually two-dimensional shapes as discussed above. The lines in the shape are called **edges**, and the edges meet at **vertices**. (Vertices is the plural of **vertex**, or corner.) It is a good idea to learn the properties of the following three-dimensional figures before taking the OGT.

THREE-DIMENSIONAL FIGURES

Figure	Description	Example
Rectangular Solid	Box with six rectangular faces; each vertex is a right angle, and the opposite faces are congruent.	
Cube	Box with six congruent square faces; each vertex is a right angle.	

(continued on next page)

THREE-DIMENSIONAL FIGURES (continued)

Square Pyramid	Base is a square; it has four triangular faces that meet at a vertex.	
Triangular Prism	Bases are two congruent triangles and sides are three rectangular faces; it has six vertices.	
Sphere	Shape is a ball and every point on the surface is the same distance from the center.	
Right Circular Cone	Base is circular; top is shaped like a cone with the vertex directly above the center of the circular base. The distance from the vertex to the circular base is the height.	
Right Circular Cylinder	Looks like a can. Top and bottom faces are parallel circles with the top one centered directly above the bottom one. The sides are made up of a rectangle wrapped around the circumference of the circle. Height is the distance from top to bottom.	

(continued on next page)

THREE-DIMENSIONAL FIGURES (continued)

Polyhedron	General term for any three-dimensional figure made up of faces with vertices and edges. Includes all of the three-dimensional figures in this table except the sphere.	

Let's Review 11: Figures

Complete each of the following questions. Use the Tip below each question to help you choose the correct answer. When you finish, check your answers at the end of this chapter.

1. **Which of the following is *not* a polyhedron?**

    A.

    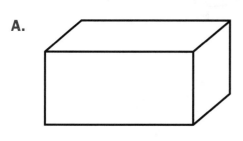

    B.

    > **TIP**
    >
    > Remember that a polyhedron has vertices and edges.

    C.

    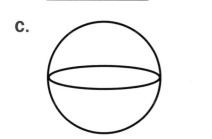

    D.

    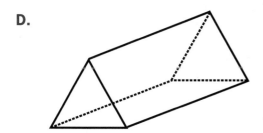

2.   **Look at the right triangle below.**

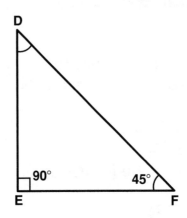

What is the measure of ∠D?

A.   30º

B.   40º

C.   45º

D.   90º

This is a right triangle, so one angle is 90º.
Remember that sum of all angles in a triangle is 180º.

3.   **Look at the regular pentagon below.**

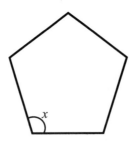

What is the measure of ∠x?

A.   108º

B.   120º

C.   135º

D.   540º

If you're unsure of the answer, go back and study
the properties of plane figures.

Lines and Angles

Lines

A **line** has an arrow on both ends to show that it keeps going.

A **line segment** is part of a line. It has two **endpoints**, one at each end, to show that it stops and doesn't keep on going in either direction.

A **ray** is also part of a line, but unlike a line segment, it keeps on going in one direction only. A ray has only one endpoint.

Lines that never intersect are called **parallel lines**. Strings on a guitar are parallel, like the lines shown here:

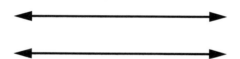

Lines that intersect to form right angles (90° angles) are called **perpendicular lines**. The place where the lines intersect is called the **point of intersection**.

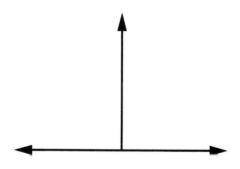

Angles

Two rays join together to form an **angle**. The place where they join is called the **vertex**.

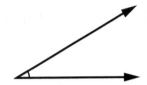

Angles can be classified by their size, usually measured in degrees. The following table shows names for angles based on their size.

TYPES OF ANGLES

Angle	Description	Example
Acute angle	Less than 90 degrees.	
Right angle	Exactly 90 degrees.	
Obtuse angle	Greater than 90 degrees and less than 180 degrees.	
Straight angle	Exactly 180 degrees.	
Reflex angle	Greater than 180 degrees	

Line and Angle Relationships

The sign ∠ stands for the word "angle."

Adjacent angles are angles that share a side. In the illustration below, ∠ADB and ∠CDB are adjacent angles.

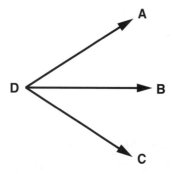

Two angles that add up to 90° are called **complementary angles**. Complementary angles that are also adjacent form a right angle. In the figure below, ∠DGE is complementary to ∠EGF. ∠DGE = 60° and ∠EGF = 30°.

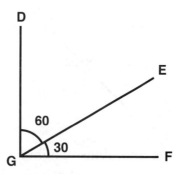

Two angles that add up to 180° are called **supplementary angles**. Supplementary angles that are also adjacent form a straight line. The angles below are supplementary. ∠HJI = 55° and ∠KJI = 125°.

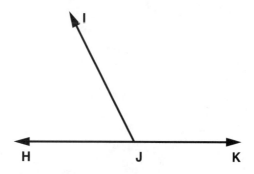

When two lines intersect, they form two pair of **vertical angles**, angles across from one another, which are always equal. In the illustration below, angles a and c are equal and angles b and d are equal.

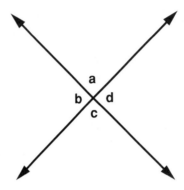

Sometimes parallel lines are intersected by a line. This intersecting line is called a **transversal** and it creates eight angles, or four pair of vertical angles. Look at the parallel lines intersected by a transversal in the figure below. Angles 1, 3, 5, and 8 are equal, and angles 2, 4, 6, and 7 are equal.

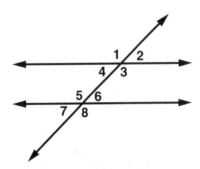

Can you see that each acute and obtuse angle formed when a transversal crosses parallel lines form supplementary angles whose sum is 180°?

Let's Review 12: Lines and Angles

Complete each of the following questions. Use the Tip below each question to help you choose the correct answer. When you finish, check your answers at the end of this chapter.

1. **What is the sum of the degree measures of two complementary angles?**

A. 80°

B. 90°

C. 120°

D. 180°

TIP

If you're not sure of the total measure of complementary angles, reread this information in the previous section of this chapter.

2. **Two streets in Josh's neighborhood run next to each other in the same direction but do not intersect. These streets are an example of what kind of lines?**

A. perpendicular

B. adjacent

C. supplementary

D. parallel

TIP

Try to remember the name for two horizontal lines that do not intersect.

Triangles

A **triangle** is a plane figure with three sides. Each of the three points on a triangle is called a vertex. You read earlier in this chapter that the sum of the angles in a triangle is 180°. Triangles are named by the measures of their angles and sides, as shown in the table on the next page.

TYPES OF TRIANGLES

Triangle	Description	Example
Equilateral triangle	Has three equal sides and three equal angles; each angle measuring 60°.	
Isosceles triangle	Has at least two equal sides and two equal angles. For example, an isosceles triangle might have angles measuring 80°-50°-50°.	
Scalene triangle	Has no equal sides and no equal angles.	
Right triangle	Has one right angle. The side across from the right angle is called the **hypotenuse**, and the other two sides are called the **legs**. The legs do not have to be equal.	
Acute triangle	Has three acute angles, which are angles less than 90°. An equilateral triangle is an acute triangle.	

(continued on next page)

TYPES OF TRIANGLES (continued)

Obtuse triangle	Has an obtuse angle, which is an angle greater than 90°. The other two angles in an obtuse triangle are acute angles.	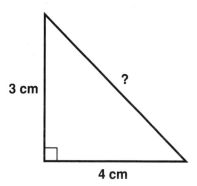

Pythagorean Theorem

The **Pythagorean theorem** is a formula used to find the length of one side of a right triangle when you know the lengths of the other two sides. The formula is $a^2 + b^2 = c^2$, where a and b are the lengths of the legs and c is the length of the hypotenuse.

Look at the triangle below.

3 cm

?

4 cm

To find the length of the hypotenuse in this triangle, substitute 3 centimeters and 4 centimeters into the formula $a^2 + b^2 = c^2$:

$$3^2 + 4^2 = c^2$$
$$c^2 = 9 + 16$$
$$c^2 = 25$$
$$c = \sqrt{25}$$

Then find the square root of 25, which is 5.

The length of the hypotenuse is 5 centimeters.

If you know the length of side c (the hypotenuse) and the length of one of the legs, you can still use the Pythagorean theorem to find the length of the missing leg. Look at this triangle:

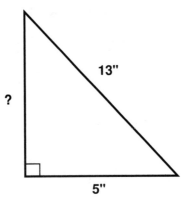

$$c^2 - a^2 = b^2$$
$$13^2 - 5^2 = b^2$$
$$b^2 = 169 - 25$$
$$b^2 = 144$$
$$b = \sqrt{144} = 12$$

So the missing side is 12 inches.

Let's Review 13: Triangles

Complete each of the following questions. Use the Tip below each question to help you choose the correct answer. When you finish, check your answers at the end of this chapter.

1.

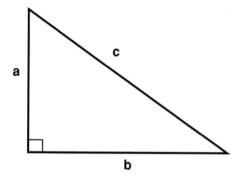

In the drawing above, the length of side *a* equals 24 inches. The length of side *c* is 26 inches. Which formula would determine the length of side *b*?

A. $a^2 + c^2 = b^2$

B. $b^2 = a^2 - c^2$

C. $a^2 - b^2 = c^2$

D. $c^2 - a^2 = b^2$

TIP

Remember that you need to put side *b* on one side of the equation.

2.   **Which of the following is an equilateral triangle?**

A.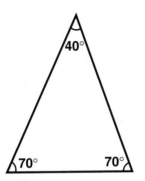

B.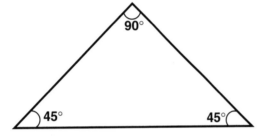

C.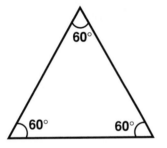

D.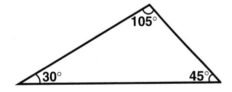

TIP

An equilateral triangle has equal sides.

3. **To help a tree grow straight, a landscaper attached a brace and a wire to the tree. He then attached the wire to a stake in the ground.**

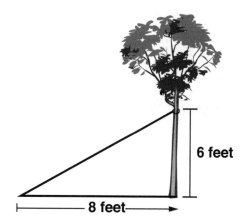

6 feet

8 feet

The brace is 6 feet from the ground and the stake is 8 feet from the base of the tree.

Find the length of the wire. (2 points)

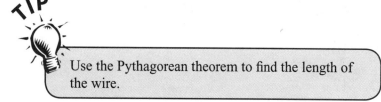

TIP

Use the Pythagorean theorem to find the length of the wire.

Chapter 5 Practice Problems

Complete each of the following practice problems. Check your answers at the end of this chapter. Be sure to read the answer explanations!

1. **The hexagon below is regular. What is the measure of each of its angles?**

    A. 90°

    B. 108°

    C. 120°

    D. 180°

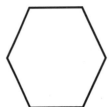

2. **An irregular octagon has a perimeter of 64. Seven of its sides measure 4, 4, 9, 8, 8, 5, and 10. What is the length of the remaining side?**

    A. 10

    B. 12

    C. 14

    D. 16

3. **What is the measure of ∠DHE in this figure?**

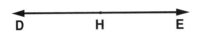

    A. 60°

    B. 90°

    C. 180°

    D. 360°

4.   Elm Street and Maple Street are parallel to each other. Walnut Street crosses Elm Street and Maple Street as shown in the figure below. What is the measure of ∠*a*?

A.   20°

B.   25°

C.   75°

D.   80°

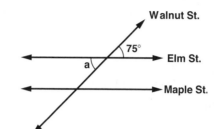

5.   Two streets in Terry's neighborhood intersect and form four right angles. These streets are an example of what kind of lines?

A.   perpendicular

B.   adjacent

C.   supplementary

D.   parallel

6.   Look at the right triangle below. What number is closest to the length of side *c*?

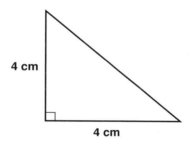

A.   4 cm

B.   6 cm

C.   8 cm

D.   16 cm

Chapter 5 Answer Explanations

Let's Review 11: Figures

1. C

A polyhedron has vertices (corners) and edges. The figure shown by answer choice C is a sphere; it has no vertices or edges, so it is not a polyhedron.

2. C

The sum of the angles of a triangle is 180°. This is a right triangle, so ∠E is 90°. If ∠F measures 45°, the remaining angle (∠D) must be 45°.

3. A

In a regular pentagon, each angle measures 108°.

Let's Review 12: Lines and Angles

1. B

Complementary angles are defined as two angles whose sum is 90°.

2. D

Lines that do not intersect are parallel.

Let's Review 13: Triangles

1. D

Since you know the measure of sides a and c, you would subtract the square of a from the square of c (the hypotenuse) to get the square of b.

2. C

An equilateral triangle has equal sides and equal 60° angles.

3. Sample answer:

$$6^2 + 8^2 = c^2$$
$$c^2 = 36 + 64$$
$$c^2 = 100$$
$$c = \sqrt{100} = 10$$

The wire is 10 feet long.

Chapter 5 Practice Problems

1. C

A regular hexagon has angles that measure 120°.

2. D

To find this answer, add all of the sides of the octagon and subtract from the perimeter.

3. C

The measure of a straight angle is 180°.

4. C

Angle a is congruent to the angle labeled 75 degrees because they are vertical angles.

5. A

Two lines that intersect to form four right angles are perpendicular.

6. B

If you use the Pythagorean theorem, you'll see that the length of side c is $\sqrt{32}$ centimeters, which is closest to 6. Note that none of the other answers will form a right triangle. Choice A would form an equilateral triangle, with 60° angles. Choices C and D are too long to form any kind of triangle with the other two sides being 4 and 4.

Chapter 6

Geometry and Spatial Sense, Part 2

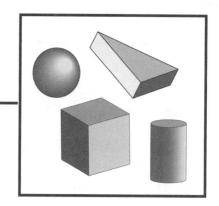

Benchmarks

D. Use coordinate geometry to represent and examine the properties of geometric figures.

E. Draw and construct representations of two- and three-dimensional geometric objects using a variety of tools, such as a straightedge, compass, and technology.

F. Represent and model transformations in a coordinate plane and describe the results.

G. Prove or disprove conjectures and solve problems involving two- and three-dimensional objects represented within a coordinate system.

H. Establish the validity of conjectures about geometric objects, their properties and relationships by counter-example, inductive and deductive reasoning, and critiquing arguments made by others.

In this chapter, you'll learn about coordinate grids. Some questions on the OGT about grids involve the movement of objects on a grid, and others involve identifying the coordinates of a figure on a grid.

In this chapter, you'll also learn how to calculate the slope of a line and how nets can be used to build three-dimensional figures.

The Coordinate Plane

A **coordinate plane** is a graph with four quadrants, usually labeled I, II, III, and IV. It has an *x*-axis and a *y*-axis. The **x-axis** is a horizontal line and the **y-axis** is a vertical line. The axes intersect at a point called the **origin**.

Look at the coordinate plane below. Find the *x*-axis and the *y*-axis and look at the different quadrants.

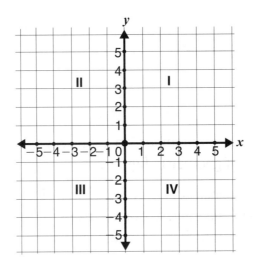

The **coordinates** of a point are like an address. They describe exactly where the point is by telling the location across or up and down from the origin. Coordinates are of the form (*x*, *y*). The *x* value always goes first.

On the OGT, you might be asked to find the coordinates of a point on the coordinate plane. To find coordinates of a point, move along the *x*-axis first. If the number of the first coordinate is positive, move to the right of the origin. If it is negative, move to the left. Then move along the *y*-axis. If the number is positive, move up from the origin. If it is negative, move down. Look at the coordinate grid shown below. Note that the coordinates of point A are (3, 4).

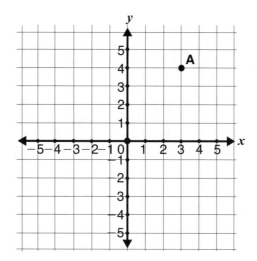

To plot a point when you know its coordinates, do the reverse. Find the x value on the *x*-axis (positive to the right of the origin and negative to the left). Then find the *y* value (positive above the origin and negative below). The point lies where these two values intersect.

Let's Review 14: The Coordinate Plane

Complete each of the following questions. Use the Tip below each question to help you choose the correct answer. When you finish, check your answers at the end of this chapter.

1. **Give the coordinates of point P on the graph below.**

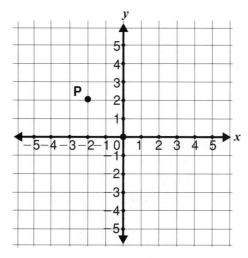

A. $(2, -2)$

B. $(0, 2)$

C. $(-2, 2)$

D. $(1, -2)$

TIP

Remember to move along the x-axis first, then move along the y-axis.

2. Look at the isosceles trapezoid below.

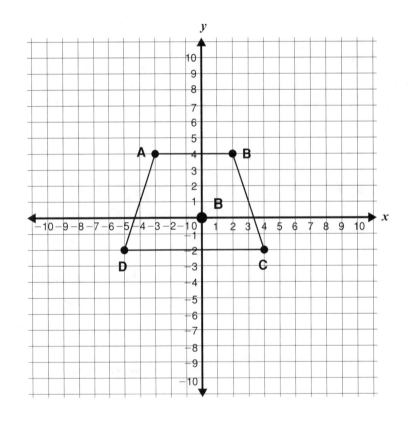

What are the coordinates of point D?

A. $(5, 2)$

B. $(-5, -2)$

C. $(-4, -2)$

D. $(-3, -2)$

TIP

The figure is an isosceles trapezoid. The *y*-coordinate of point D will be the same as point C.

3. **Which point on the graph below has the coordinates $(-4, -2)$**

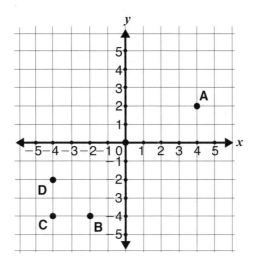

A. point A

B. point B

C. point C

D. point D

TIP

Remember to move along the *x*-axis first.

4. Three of the vertices of a quadrilateral are (1, 3), (5, 3), and (4, −1).

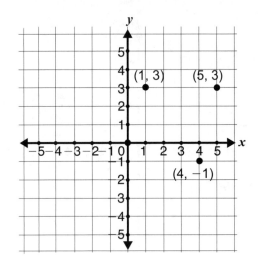

When used as the last vertex, which point would make the quadrilateral a rhombus?

A. $(1, -1)$

B. $(0, -1)$

C. $(-1, -1)$

D. $(-2, -1)$

TIP

A rhombus has four equal sides.

Transformations

Transformations involve the movement of figures on a coordinate plane. On the OGT, you might be asked to choose the correct coordinates of a figure moved in a certain way on the coordinate plane. The following are some common transformations:

Rotation

When you rotate a figure, you move it around a fixed point, which is called the center of rotation. A rotation can be large or small. A rotation of 180° is called a half-turn. A rotation of 90° is called a quarter turn. If you think of the figure as being rigidly attached to the end of the minute hand of a clock, you can see how its orientation will change as it is being rotated.

R · Я

R · ᴚ

Reflection

When a figure is reflected, it is flipped across a line, which may or may not be visible. Think of the reflection of a figure as a mirror image, where the "line" is the mirror. On a figure to be reflected, the line may be drawn with the figure, or you may just have to imagine it.

R | Я

Translation

A translation is a slide. A figure that is translated is moved as if it were sliding in one direction. It doesn't get rotated or flipped.

R → R

R ↘ R

Let's Review 15: Figure Transformations

Complete each of the following questions. Use the Tip below each question to help you choose the correct answer. When you finish, check your answers at the end of this chapter.

1. **Triangle ABC has vertices with coordinates A (1, 6), B (3, 10), and C (5, 6).**

   Draw and label triangle ABC on the grid provided.

   Draw triangle A′B′C′ by translating each vertex of the triangle two units to the right and two units down. Appropriately label triangle A′B′C′.

   Draw a triangle A″B″C″ formed by reflecting triangle ABC across the *x*-axis. (4 points)

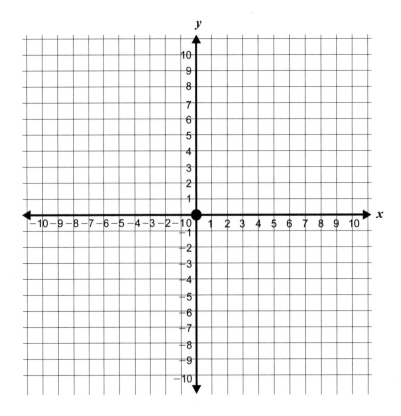

2. **Moving a geometric figure around a fixed point is transformation by**

A. sliding.

B. reflection.

C. rotation.

D. translation.

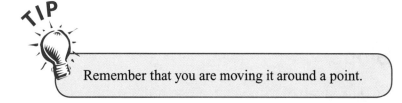

TIP

Remember that you are moving it around a point.

3. **Look at the figure below and how it looks after it is moved. Determine which transformation, if any, of Figure I is shown in Figure II?**

$$A \rightarrow A$$

A. rotation

B. reflection

C. translation

D. no transformation

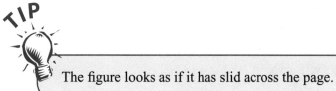

TIP

The figure looks as if it has slid across the page.

Nets

A **net** is a plane figure that can be folded into a three-dimensional shape. Sometimes you will be able to tell by the shape of a net what figure it will be when it is folded. Other times, you will have to count the faces and the corners. Look at this net:

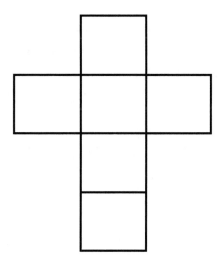

Notice the details in the net. The figure has six square faces that are same size. What three-dimensional figure has six square faces that are the same size? If you said a cube, you're correct!

Slope

The **slope** of a line indicates a line's steepness; the greater the slope, the steeper the line. The slope of a line can be positive, negative, zero, or undefined.

Lines with a positive slope slant upward from left to right. Lines with a negative slope slant downward from left to right. A slope of zero means the line is horizontal, parallel to the x-axis; it is not steep at all! An undefined slope is one that cannot be determined because you cannot divide by zero. A line with an undefined slope is vertical and parallel to the y-axis.

The **x-intercept** of a line is the pair of coordinates at which a line crosses the x-axis (where $y = 0$), and the **y-intercept** is the pair of coordinates at which a line crosses the y-axis (where $x = 0$).

To determine the slope of a line, use this formula, which is called the **rise-over-run formula:**

$$\text{Slope} = \frac{y_2 - y_1}{x_2 - x_1},$$

which uses the values of two points on the line, (x_1, y_1) and (x_2, y_2).

For example, suppose you want to find the slope of a line that has points at coordinates $(1, 5)$ and $(4, -3)$. You would use the formula this way:

$$\text{Slope} = \frac{(y_2 - y_1)}{(x_2 - x_1)}$$

$$= \frac{(-3 - 5)}{(4 - 1)} = -\frac{8}{3}$$

So the slope of this line is $\frac{-8}{3}$.

Let's Review 16: Nets and Slope

Complete each of the following questions. Use the Tip below each question to help you choose the correct answer. When you finish, check your answers at the end of this chapter.

1. **Which of the following describes the slope of a line parallel to the** *x*-**axis?**

A. positive slope

B. negative slope

C. zero slope

D. undefined slope

TIP

If you don't remember what you learned about slope, reread this section to find the answer.

2. **What is the slope of a line that passes through the points (2, 5) and (6, 13)?**

A. −2

B. 0

C. 1

D. 2

TIP

Use the rise-over-run formula to find the slope of this line.

3. **The figure below shows the net for a three-dimensional object.**

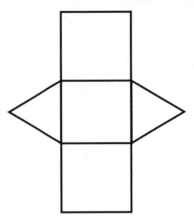

When folded, which object will this net produce?

A.

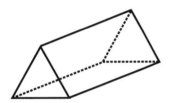

B.

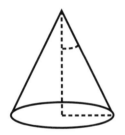

C.

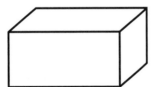

D.

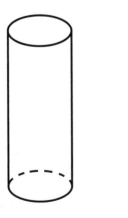

TIP

Look carefully at the parts of the net that would be the bases. Then look at how the other shapes would connect to the bases.

Chapter 6 Practice Problems

Complete each of the following practice problems. Check your answers at the end of this chapter. Be sure to read the answer explanations!

1. The vertices of a quadrilateral are (−8, −3), (−5, −3), (−3, −5), and (−10, −5).

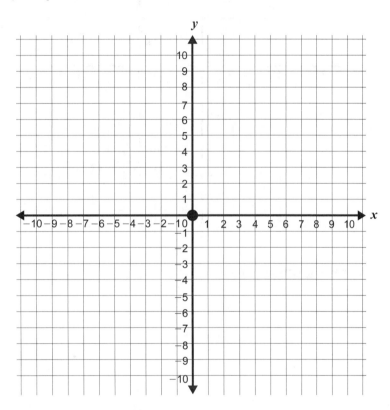

    Which describes this quadrilateral?

A. parallelogram

B. rectangle

C. rhombus

D. trapezoid

2. Cheryl is designing a wallpaper border. She is reflecting rectangle ABCD over the *x*-axis on the coordinate plane to create rectangle A′B′C′D′.

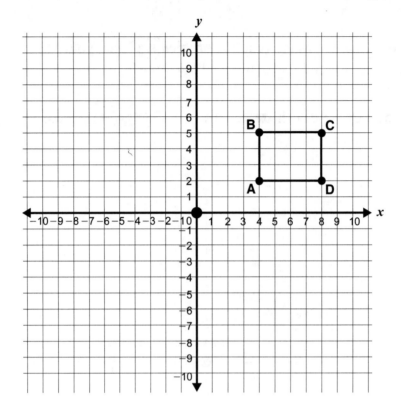

What are the coordinates of C′?

A. $(8, -5)$

B. $(5, -8)$

C. $(8, 2)$

D. $(-8, -2)$

3. Which is the slope of a line that passes through the points (2, 4) and (−7, 10)?

A. $\dfrac{2}{3}$

B. $-\dfrac{2}{3}$

C. 2

D. −2

4. An art student is making geometric designs for a special project.
    She plots the coordinates of the vertices of a rectangle on a grid.
    The first three coordinates are (3, 2), (3, 5), and (8, 5). What are the
    coordinates of the fourth vertex?

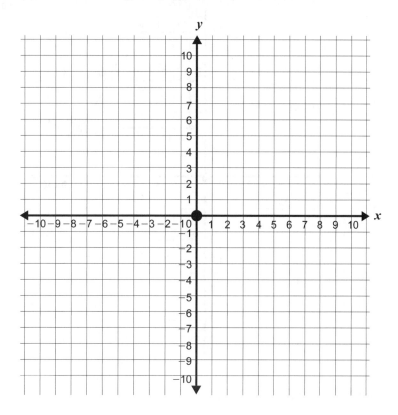

A. (2, 8)

B. (3, 8)

C. (8, 2)

D. (8, 3)

5. **Four points are connected with line segments, as shown on the coordinate plane below.**

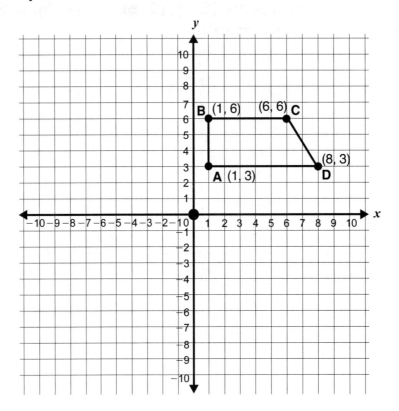

Find the slope of each side.

Determine whether the shape is a trapezoid. Show your work or provide an explanation of your answer. (4 points)

6. Jane needs to make a model of an ice-cream cone for art class. She plans to cut a shape out of posterboard and then fold it to make a cone with a round base and a pointed top. Which of these nets or shapes could Jane use to make her model?

A.

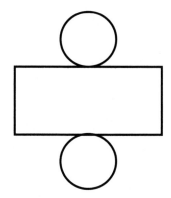

B.

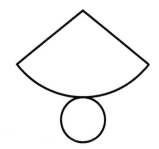

C.

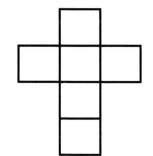

D.

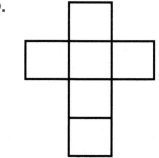

Chapter 6 Answer Explanations

Let's Review 14: The Coordinate Plane

1. C

To get to Point P, you have to move to -2 on the x-axis and 2 on the y-axis.

2. B

Point D has to have the same y value as point C for this to be an isosceles trapezoid. The x-value can be determined from the grid.

3. D

If you move to -4 on the x-axis and -2 on the y-axis, you will get to point D.

4. B

A rhombus has four equal sides. If you count blocks on the grid, you'll see that the correct answer is B: $(0, -1)$

Let's Review 15: Figure Transformations

1.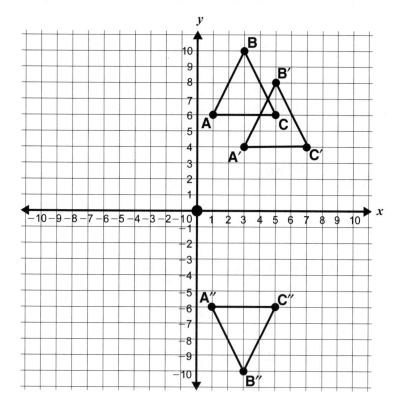

2. C

If you weren't sure of this answer, you could figure it out by using the process of elimination. It is not a reflection or mirror image. It's not a translation, which is a slide. It's a rotation.

3. C

When you slide a shape without flipping or rotating it, it's called a translation.

Let's Review 16: Nets and Slopes

1. C

Flat horizontal lines have a slope of zero (no rise at all).

2. D

When you substitute the coordinates into the rise-over-run formula, you'll see that the slope is $\frac{(13-5)}{(6-2)} = \frac{8}{4} = 2$.

3. A

This net has triangular bases and sides that are squares. It's a triangular prism.

Chapter 6 Practice Problems

1. D

This figure is a trapezoid, a shape with one pair of parallel sides.

2. A

The coordinates of point C are (8, 5). When you reflect the rectangle over the x-axis, the coordinates of C' are (8, −5).

3. B

Use the formula $\frac{(y_2-y_1)}{(x_2-x_1)} = \frac{(10-4)}{(-7-2)} = \frac{6}{-9} = -\frac{2}{3}$.

4. C

A rectangle has two pairs of equal sides. Therefore, the correct coordinates are (8, 2).

5. Sample answer:

To find the slope of a line, use the formula $\frac{(y_2-y_1)}{(x_2-x_1)}$.

For the first side, AB, substitute the coordinates like this: $\frac{(6-3)}{(1-1)}$; the slope is undefined (you cannot divide by 0). Therefore, that side is vertical. Then substitute the coordinates from the opposite side, CD, into the formula: $\frac{(3-6)}{(8-6)} = \frac{-3}{2}$. Since the slopes are not the same, that pair of sides is not parallel. Then check the other two sides.

For BC, $\frac{(6-6)}{(6-1)} = 0$, and for AD, $\frac{(3-3)}{(8-1)} = 0$. So these sides have the same slope and are parallel. The figure is a trapezoid because it has only one pair of parallel sides.

6. B

The net shown in answer choice B has a circle for the base, and can be folded into a shape with a point, which is a cone.

Chapter 7

Measurement

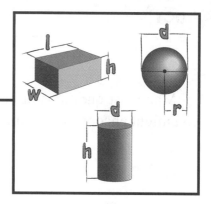

Benchmarks

A. Solve increasingly complex non-routine measurement problems and check for reasonableness of results.

B. Use formulas to find surface area and volume for specified three-dimensional objects accurate to a specified level of precision.

C. Apply indirect measurement techniques, tools, and formulas, as appropriate, to find perimeter, circumference and area of circles, triangles, quadrilaterals, and composite shapes, and to find volumes of prisms, cylinders, and pyramids.

D. Use proportional reasoning and apply indirect measurement techniques, including right triangle trigonometry and properties of similar triangles, to solve problems involving measurements and rates.

E. Estimate and compute various attributes, including length, angle measure, area, surface area, and volume, to a specified level or precision.

F. Write and solve real-word, multi-step problems involving money, elapsed time, and temperature, and verify reasonableness of solutions.

In this chapter, you will learn about measurement, building on what you learned in the two chapters on Geometry and Spatial Sense. You will work with plane figures again, but this time you'll learn how to find the perimeter and area of these figures. You'll also learn how to find the volume and surface area of three-dimensional figures in this chapter.

Many test questions on the OGT will involve real-life situations similar to those you might encounter at home, at work, or in school.

Similar Figures

Congruent figures are exactly the same shape and size. You could place one congruent figure on top of another and it would fit perfectly. **Similar figures** are not necessarily congruent. Similar figures have the same shape but not the same size. If figures are congruent, the sign ≅ is used, as in ΔKLM ≅ ΔNOP.

If figures are similar, the ~ sign is used, as in ΔKLM ~ ΔNOP.

If figures are similar, their corresponding sides can be written as a proportion because one figure is an enlargement of the other.

These triangles are similar:

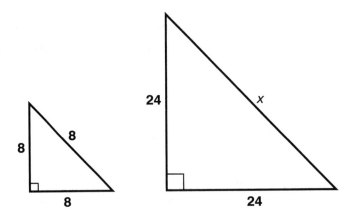

These rectangles are similar:

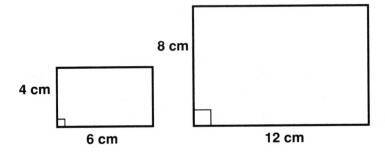

Note that the ratios of the corresponding sides of these rectangles are the same when they are reduced:

$$4:8 = 1:2$$
$$6:12 = 1:2$$

This proportionality property lets you determine the missing side for similar triangles. For example, read this question:

Find the missing length (x) for the pair of similar triangles below.

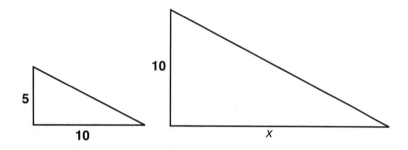

Remember that corresponding sides of similar figures have dimensions that can be expressed as the same ratio, meaning they are proportional. The ratio for the heights is:

$$5 : 10 = 1 : 2$$

For the lengths, the ratio should be the same because they are similar triangles. Thus,

$$10 : x = 1 : 2$$

and therefore $x = 20$

Let's Review 17: Similar Figures

Complete each of the following questions. Use the Tip below each question to help you choose the correct answer. When you finish, check your answers at the end of this chapter.

1. Jamie drew a rectangle that measures **12** inches in width and **24** inches in length. If Jamie enlarges the rectangle so that it is **2** feet wide, how long will the rectangle be?

    A. 2 feet

    B. 4 feet

    C. 6 feet

    D. 8 feet

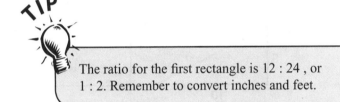

TIP

The ratio for the first rectangle is 12 : 24 , or 1 : 2. Remember to convert inches and feet.

2. Rebecca is designing a wallpaper border. The pattern for one part is shown below. The units of measurement are centimeters.

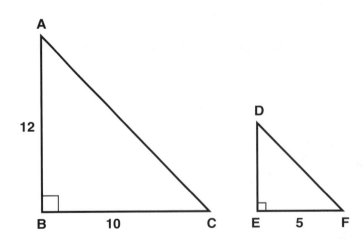

Triangles ABC and DEF are similar.

Determine the length of side DE. Show your work or provide an explanation to support your answer. (2 points)

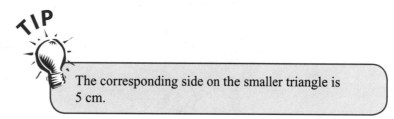

TIP

The corresponding side on the smaller triangle is 5 cm.

3. If the two equilateral triangles shown below are similar, find the measure of side *x*.

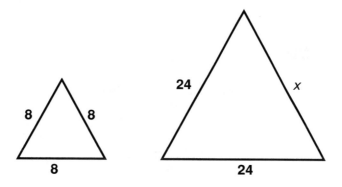

A. 8

B. 12

C. 24

D. 48

TIP

Both triangles are equilateral; this means that all sides are equal. What is the proportion between the two triangles?

Perimeter

The **perimeter** is the distance around a plane figure. As you saw in the chapters on Geometry and Spatial Sense, a **plane figure** is a flat, closed figure. The perimeter is commonly measured in inches, feet, centimeters, or meters.

Find the perimeter of the hexagon shown below:

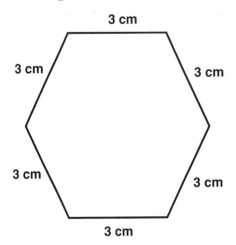

To find the perimeter, add all of the sides $3 + 3 + 3 + 3 + 3 + 3 = 18$, or $6 \times 3 = 18$ cm.

Circumference

The perimeter of a circle is called its **circumference**. Use this formula to find a circle's circumference:

$$C = \pi \times d,$$

where π (pi, pronounced "pie") is approximately 3.14, and d is the diameter.

Look at this circle:

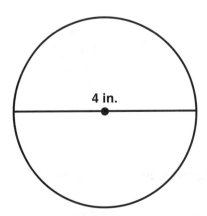

To find the circumference of the circle shown above, multiply π (or 3.14) $\times$ the diameter, 4. Then round to the nearest whole number. The circumference is 13 inches.

Sometimes only the radius of a circle is given. When this happens, you have to double the radius because the diameter is twice the radius. Look at the circle below.

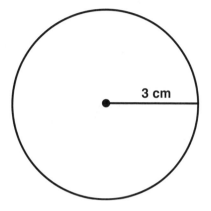

To find the circumference of this circle, first double the radius to find the diameter: $3 \times 2 = 6$. Then use the formula $C = \pi \times$ diameter.

$$C = (3.14) \times 6$$
$$C = 19 \text{ cm}$$

Central Angles

Angles can be formed inside a circle when two radii meet at the center of the circle. The center is the vertex of this angle, and the angle is called a **central angle**. Look at the circle below. It has two central angles, A and B.

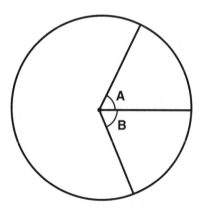

To determine the measures of central angles in a circle, remember that a circle is 360°, so the total measure of all of the central angles cannot be more than 360°. Half of a circle measures 180°. For example, in the circle below, you can figure out the measure of the missing angle, which is 130°, by subtracting the sum of the measures of the other central angles from 360°.

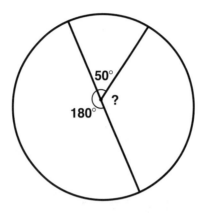

Let's Review 18: Perimeter and Central Angles

Complete each of the following questions. Use the Tip below each question to help you choose the correct answer. When you finish, check your answers at the end of this chapter.

1. **The perimeters of the two triangles are equal. What is the length of the third side in the second triangle?**

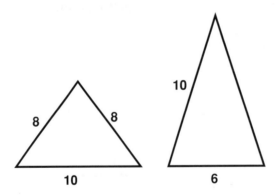

A. 4

B. 6

C. 8

D. 10

TIP

Add the sides of the first triangle to find the perimeter, which is also the perimeter of the second triangle.

2. A hexagon has a perimeter of 25. The lengths of five of its sides are
    3, 3, 4, 6, and 6. What is the length of the remaining side?

A. 2

B. 3

C. 4

D. 5

TIP

The perimeter is the sum of the lengths of all six sides.

3. Look at the clock shown below.

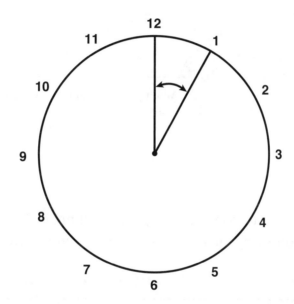

What is the approximate measure of the central angle shown?

A. 12°

B. 15°

C. 30°

D. 36°

TIP

An entire circle measures 360°. This central angle is
one of 12 equal parts.

4. **Kelly has an irregularly shaped backyard with five sides as shown below.**

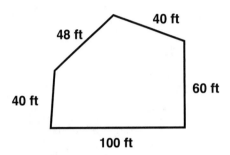

What is the perimeter of his backyard?

A. 188 feet

B. 248 feet

C. 288 feet

D. 388 feet

Add together the sides of Kelly's yard to solve this problem.

Area

The area of a figure is a measure of the space the entire object covers. The formulas for area listed in the following table are also on the reference sheet:

AREA

Figure	Formula	Example
Rectangle	Area = *lw*	*w* [rectangle] *l*

(continued on next page)

AREA (continued)

Triangle	Area $= \frac{1}{2} bh$	
Trapezoid	Area $= \frac{1}{2} h(b_1 + b_2)$	
Parallelogram	Area $= bh$	
Circle	Area $= \pi r^2$	

Look at the rectangle below:

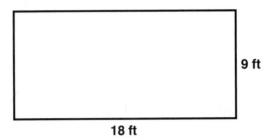

9 ft

18 ft

To find the area of this rectangle, substitute the length and width into the formula you just learned:

$$A = lw$$
$$A = 18 \text{ feet} \times 9 \text{ feet}$$
$$A = 162 \text{ square feet}$$

Notice that the area is expressed in square feet.

Now look at this circle:

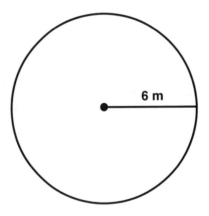

6 m

To find the area of this circle, place the radius into the formula you just learned, which is usually given to you on the OGT. Use 3.14 for π, and round your answer to the nearest whole number.

$$A = \pi r^2$$
$$A = (3.14) \times 6^2$$
$$A = (3.14) \times 36$$
$$A = 113 \text{ square meters}$$

Volume

Volume is the measure of the amount of space inside of something. To find the volume or capacity of a three-dimensional figure, use the formulas in the following table, which are also on your reference sheet:

VOLUME

Figure	Volume	Example
Rectangular solid, or rectangular prism	$V = lwh$	
Cylinder	$V = \pi r^2 h$	
Cone	$V = \frac{1}{3}\pi r^2 h$	

(continued on next page)

VOLUME (continued)

Square Pyramid	$V = \frac{1}{3}Bh$	
Sphere	$V = \frac{4}{3}\pi r^3$	

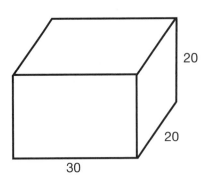

To find the volume of the rectangular prism above, substitute the measurements of the length, width, and height into the formula you just learned:

$$V = lwh$$
$$V = 30 \times 20 \times 20$$
$$V = 12,000$$

The volume of the rectangular prism is 12,000 cubic centimeters.

To find the volume of a cylinder, you would use the formula $V = \pi r^2 h$. To find the volume of a cylinder with a radius of 3 and a height of 5, substitute these values into the formula:

$$V = (3.14)3^2 \times 5$$
$$V = (3.14) \times 9 \times 5$$
$$V = 141$$

Surface Area

Surface area refers to the area of all the surfaces that make up a three-dimensional figure. If you imagine the figure flattened into nets, as discussed in the previous chapter, you can see that the total surface area for a rectangular prism and a right circular cylinder are given by these formulas:

Rectangular prism:　　S.A. $= 2(lw) + 2(hw) + 2(lh)$

Each term represents the area of two congruent sides.

Right circular cylinder: S.A. $= 2\pi rh + 2\pi r^2$

The first term is the area of the side that wraps around the cylinder. Can you see that its length is the circumference of the circular end? The second term is the area of the two circular ends.

To find the surface area of a rectangular prism with a height of 6 cm, a length of 8 cm, and a width of 2 cm, use the formula shown above:

S.A. $= 2(lw) + 2(hw) + 2(lh)$

S.A. $= 2(8 \times 2) + 2 (6 \times 2) + 2 (8 \times 6)$

S.A. $= 2(16) + 2(12) + 2(48)$

S.A. $= 32 + 24 + 96$

S.A. $= 152$ square centimeters

Multi-step Problems

Some measurement questions on the OGT will ask you to solve problems involving money, time, or temperature that require more than one step. Read this problem:

Melissa earns $7.00 per hour at her job. Her employer must pay her "time and a half" ($1\frac{1}{2}$ times her regular hourly earnings) for each hour over 40 hours per week. Her employer withholds 12% of her gross pay for various taxes. Melissa worked 42 hours this week. What is the amount of her paycheck, after taxes are withheld?

To answer this problem, you first need to determine how much Melissa earned for working 40 hours:

$$\$7.00 \times 40 \text{ hours} = \$280$$

Now determine how much money Melissa is paid per hour in overtime:

$$\$7.00 \times 1.5 = \$10.5$$

Next determine her overtime pay; Melissa worked two hours of overtime.

$$\$10.5 \times 2 = \$21.00$$

Add her regular pay and her overtime pay:

$$\$280 + \$21 = \$301$$

Now, determine the amount withheld for taxes:

$$\$301 \times 12\% = \$36.12$$

Subtract this amount from the amount of money Melissa earned:

$$\$301 - \$36.12 = \$264.88$$

Let's Review 19: Area and Volume

Complete each of the following questions. Use the Tip below each question to help you choose the correct answer. When you finish, check your answers with those at the end of the chapter.

1. **What is the volume of the box pictured below?**

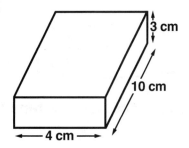

A. 17 cubic centimeters

B. 40 cubic centimeters

C. 70 cubic centimeters

D. 120 cubic centimeters

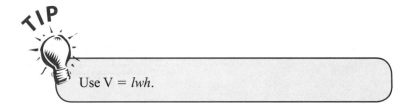

TIP

Use $V = lwh$.

2. **A rotating sprinkler is used to water a yard. The radius of the area being sprayed is 8 feet. What is the wet area of the yard?**

A. 20 square feet

B. 25 square feet

C. 64 square feet

D. 201 square feet

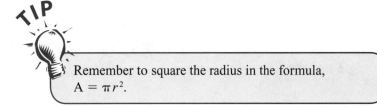

TIP

Remember to square the radius in the formula, $A = \pi r^2$.

3. **A storage tank below has a radius of 8 feet and a height of 10 feet.**

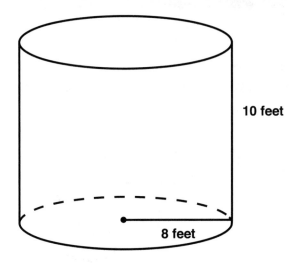

10 feet

8 feet

What is the surface area of the storage tank?

A. 402 square feet

B. 455 square feet

C. 502 square feet

D. 904 square feet

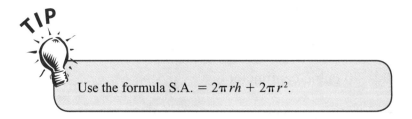

TIP

Use the formula S.A. $= 2\pi rh + 2\pi r^2$.

4. **Melissa is going on a business trip to Florida. Her first flight leaves Philadelphia at 8:30 a.m., but she must be at the airport 60 minutes prior to her flight. Her plane arrives in Georgia at 11:00 a.m. Here she will take a 12:30 p.m. flight to Tampa, Florida. This flight is scheduled to land in Tampa at 2:00 p.m.**

Determine the amount of time it takes Melissa to get to Tampa, Florida, beginning with the time she must arrive at the airport in Philadelphia and ending with the time her plane lands in Tampa, Florida. (2 points)

Chapter 7 Practice Problems

Complete each of the following practice problems. Check your answers with the Answer Key at the end of this chapter. Be sure to read the answer explanations!

1. **What is the volume of the box pictured below?**

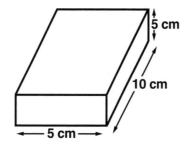

   A. 15 cubic centimeters

   B. 25 cubic centimeters

   C. 125 cubic centimeters

   D. 250 cubic centimeters

2. **Emile wants to wrap the box below with wrapping paper. How many square inches of wrapping paper does he need?**

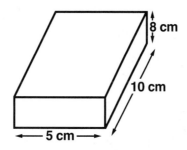

   A. 100 square centimeters

   B. 160 square centimeters

   C. 340 square centimeters

   D. 420 square centimeters

3. **Paul wants to close off a rectangular area in his backyard so that he can leave his dog outside. He buys enough grass seed to cover 168 square feet.**

   If the length of the enclosure is 14 feet, what is the width?

   A. 12 feet

   B. 14 feet

   C. 16 feet

   D. 18 feet

4. **The volume of a cylinder is found by using the formula V = $\pi r^2 h$. How do the volumes of cylinder A and cylinder B compare?**

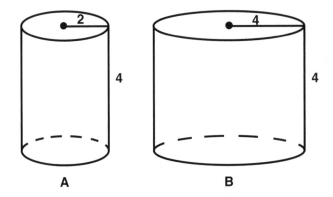

   A. The volume of cylinder A is larger.

   B. The volume of cylinder B is larger.

   C. It is not possible to compare the volumes.

   D. The volumes of cylinder A and cylinder B are the same.

5. Rory is 6 feet tall. He casts a shadow that measures 8 feet long at the same time that a tree in the park casts a shadow that is 16 feet long. What is the approximate height of the tree?

A. 12 feet

B. 13.5 feet

C. 15 feet

D. 18.5 feet

6. What is the area of a circle with a radius of 10 cm?

A. 3.14 square centimeters

B. 31.4 square centimeters

C. 314 square centimeters

D. 3,140 square centimeters

7. Rounding off to the nearest centimeter, what is the volume of the box pictured below?

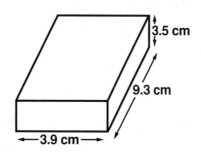

A. 17 cubic centimeters

B. 13 cubic centimeters

C. 36 cubic centimeters

D. 127 cubic centimeters

8. **The diagram below shows the dimensions of a wall that needs to be painted. The door represented by the shaded rectangle is not to be painted.**

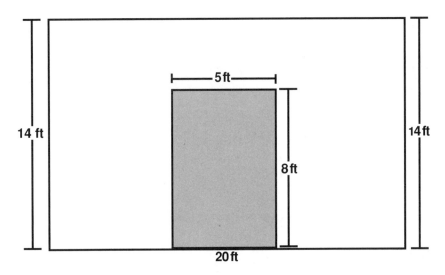

Determine the area, to the nearest square foot, of the wall that is to be painted. Show your work or provide an explanation for your answer. (2 points)

9. **Gretchen earns $10.50 an hour at her summer job. Her employer must pay her "time and a half" ($1\frac{1}{2}$ times her regular hourly earnings) for each hour over 40 hours per week. Her employer withholds 15% of her gross pay for various taxes. The table shows Gretchen's work time for the week.**

Gretchen's Hour

Mon	Tues	Wed	Thu	Fri
$9\frac{1}{2}$ h	8 h	$8\frac{1}{2}$ h	$9\frac{3}{4}$ h	$10\frac{1}{4}$ h

Determine the amount of Gretchen's pay check, after taxes are withheld, for the week shown in the table. Show your work or provide an explanation to support your answer. (4 points)

Chapter 7 Answer Explanations

Let's Review 17: Similar Figures

1. B

The ratio for the widths is 12 : 24 = 1 : 2. The length of the second rectangle will have to be 4 feet to keep that same ratio: 24 : x = 1 : 2, so x = 48 inches, or 4 feet.

2. Sample answer:

The smaller triangle is half the size of the first. You can tell this because side BC has a length of 10 centimeters and side EF has a length of 5 centimeters. Therefore the ratio between the triangles is 2 : 1. Line DE is the height of the smaller triangle. The larger triangle has a height of 12 centimeters, so the smaller triangle has a height of 6 centimeters (ratio of 2 : 1).

3. C

The ratio for these triangles is 1:3 and the corresponding side of the smaller triangle is 8, so the correct answer is 24.

Let's Review 18: Perimeter and Central Angles

1. D

The perimeter of the first triangle is 26. The second triangle has the same perimeter, but we are only given two of the sides, which add up to 16. Therefore, the last side must be 10.

2. B

The sides of the hexagon add up to 22 and its perimeter is 25. Therefore, the missing side must be 3.

3. C

An entire circle measures 360°. This circle is divided into twelve equal parts and the central angle shown is one of those parts. Therefore, you need to divide 12 into 360. The answer is 30°.

4. C

To find the perimeter of Kelly's backyard, you have to add the sides: $100 + 40 + 60 + 48 + 40$. His yard has a perimeter of 288 feet.

Let's Review 19: Area and Volume

1. D

When you multiply 10 by 4 by 3, you get 120.

2. D

To solve this problem, you need to find the area of a circle with a radius of 8 feet. If you substitute this into the formula $A = \pi r^2$, the answer is 201 square feet.

3. D

When you plug in the values for the formula for surface area: S.A. $= 2\pi rh + 2\pi r^2$, it looks like this: $2(3.14) \times 8 \times 10 + 2(3.14) \times 8^2$. When you solve the equation, the answer is 904 square feet.

4. Sample answer:

Melissa's first flight leaves at 8:30 and lands at 11:00. This flight is $2\frac{1}{2}$ hours long and Melissa had to be at the airport one hour prior to the flight, so her travel time, up to this point, is $3\frac{1}{2}$ hours. Her next flight doesn't leave until 12:30, so you need to add $1\frac{1}{2}$ to her travel time. She has traveled 5 hours so far. This flight lasts $1\frac{1}{2}$ hours, so Melissa's travel time is $6\frac{1}{2}$ hours.

Chapter 7 Practice Problems

1. D

Substitute the values in the formula for the volume of rectangular solid: V = *lwh*; V = 5 × 5 × 10. V = 250 cubic centimeters.

2. C

To determine how much wrapping paper Emile needs, substitute the dimensions of the box into the formula to find the surface are of a rectangular square: S.A. = 2(*lw*) + 2(*hw*) + 2(*lh*); S.A. = 2(8 × 10) + 2(10 × 5) + 2(8 × 5); S.A. = 2(80) + 2(50) + 2(40); S.A. = 160 + 100 + 80. S.A. = 340 square centimeters.

3. A

To find the area of a rectangle, you multiply length by width. This problem gives us the area (168 square feet) and the length (14 feet). You need to divide 14 into 168 to get the answer.

4. B

The volume of cylinder A is about 50; the volume is cylinder B is about 200.

5. A

Set up a ratio to solve this problem:

$6 : x = 8 : 16$.

Cross-multiply to get $8x = 96$, or $x = 12$ feet.

6. C

When you plug the radius of 10 cm into the formula $A = \pi r^2$, the answer is 3.14 × 10 × 10 = 314 square centimeters.

7. **D**

When you multiply the length, width, and height of the box, the answer is about 127 cubic centimeters.

8. **Sample answer:**

To determine the area of the wall, you need to multiply the length, 20 feet by the height, 14 feet. The area of the entire wall is 280 square feet. Next you need to subtract the area of the door. The area of the door is $8 \times 5 = 40$ square feet. Therefore, the area of the wall without the door is 240 square feet.

9. **Sample answer:**

First, you have to add up the hours that Gretchen worked during the week. She worked 46 hours. Next, figure out her pay for 40 hours, $40 \times \$10.5 = \$420$. Next determine her overtime pay per hour: $1\frac{1}{2} \times 10.5 = \$15.75$. Then her overtime pay is $6 \times \$15.75 = \$94.50$. Add the two amounts: $\$420 + \$94.50 = \$514.50$. Then determine how much money her employer withholds: $\$514.50 \times 15\% = \$77.18$. Then subtract this from Gretchen's gross pay to get the amount of her paycheck: $\$437.32$.

Chapter 8

Patterns, Functions, and Algebra

$$40x^2$$
$$7(6x)+x$$
$$17-5<20$$

Benchmarks

A. Generalize and explain patterns and sequences in order to find the next term and the nth term.

B. Identify and classify functions as linear or nonlinear, and contrast their properties using tables, graphs, or equations.

C. Translate information from one representation (words, table, graph, or equation) to another representation of a relation or function.

D. Use algebraic representations, such as tables, graphs, expressions, functions and inequalities, to model and solve problem situations.

E. Analyze and compare functions and their graphs using attributes, such as rates of change, intercepts, and zeros.

F. Solve and graph linear equations and inequalities.

G. Solve quadratic equations with real roots by graphing, formula, and factoring.

H. Solve systems of linear equations involving two variables graphically and symbolically.

I. Model and solve problem situations involving direct and inverse variation.

J. Describe and interpret rates of change from graphical and numerical data.

171

In this chapter, you'll learn how to answer questions on the OGT about expressions and equations. You will learn how to choose the expression or equation that could be used to solve a real-life problem.

You'll see that some expressions and equations have more than one variable, and some are displayed in table form. An inequality shows the relation between two values. You'll learn about inequalities in this chapter, and you'll also learn about functions.

Expressions

In algebra, letters often stand for numbers that need to be determined. These letters are called **variables.** Any number in front of a variable means that the variable will be multiplied by that number. For example, $2x$ means that x will be multiplied by 2. Keep in mind that any variable, such as x or y, has a 1 before it even though the 1 is not written. In other words, $x = 1x$ and $y = 1y$.

Algebraic **expressions** are simply terms that contain variables. Parentheses are often used in algebraic expressions. Remember that the order of computation is parentheses first, then multiplication and division, then addition and subtraction. Look at this expression:

$2(x + y)$. This means that the 2 multiplies everything inside the parentheses, so the expression is equal to $2x + 2y$.

To simplify an expression such as

$$4(3x) + x$$

begin by multiplying, to get

$$12x + x$$

Now simplify the expression even further by adding (remember that x is the same as $1x$) to get:

$$13x$$

You can write expressions based on a given real-world situation. Read this question:

Mabel bought 12 pencils for 20 cents each, 6 pens for 50 cents each, 2 erasers for 50 cents each, and 5 sheets of construction paper for 20 cents each. Which expression would enable Mabel to find out how much money she spent?

Add the costs, item by item:

$$12(20) + 6(50) + 2(50) + 5(20)$$

and then combine like items (items with the same cost) to get:

$$17(20) + 8(50)$$

Let's try one more:

Abraham uses the expression $7x + 10.5y$ to determine the amount he earns at a pay rate of seven dollars an hour plus time and a half for overtime. One week he worked 40 hours plus 2 hours of overtime.

The information in this problem gives you the values to substitute for x and y. Substitute 40 for x, the number of regular hours Abraham worked, and substitute 2 for y, the number of overtime hours Abraham worked. This expression would help Abraham determine how much money he would earn in a week.

$$7(40) + 10.5(2)$$

Equations

An algebraic **equation** is a statement that says two values are equal. You can spot an equation easily because it has an equal sign, which separates the two sides of the equation. Look at this equation:

$$t + 45 = 100$$

In this equation, t is the variable, which represents the unknown quantity. You can solve the equation, and find the value of t, by subtracting 45 from each side of the equation as shown here:

$$t + 45 - 45 = 100 - 45$$
$$t = 55$$

Remember that for an equation to stay *equal*, whatever you do to one side, you must also do to the other side.

Sometimes you might be asked to choose the correct equation based on a situation. Read this problem:

Terry's take-home (net) pay is his gross pay minus the $175 his employer deducts each week for taxes. His net pay is $500 a week. Write an equation that could be used to find Terry's gross pay.

Terry's gross pay is the unknown variable, which will be represented by x. This equation could be used to determine Terry's gross pay:

$$x - \$175 = \$500$$

To solve this equation and determine Terry's gross pay, put x, the variable, on a side by itself by adding $175 to each side of the equation:

$$x - \$175 + \$175 = \$500 + \$175, \text{ or}$$
$$x = \$675$$

Some equations have more than one variable. When solving an equation such as $2x + y = 10$, you usually are solving for y in terms of x. In other words, you are finding an expression for y that involves x.

To solve this equation, move everything except y to the opposite side of the equation.

$$2x + y = 10$$
$$y = 10 - 2x$$

Let's try another one. This time, solve for b in terms of a.

$$4b = 16a$$

Divide both sides by 4:

$$\frac{4b}{4} = \frac{16a}{4}, \text{ or}$$
$$b = 4a$$

Equations with more than one variable are sometimes written in table form. The table below shows the values of x and y for the equation $3x - y = 0$.

x	y
2	6
3	9
4	12
5	15
6	?

What value of y makes the equation true when $x = 6$?

If you substitute 6 for x, the equation looks like this: $3(6) - y = 0$. You could probably figure this out in your head. However, the equation can also be solved this way:

$$18 - y = 0$$
$$y = 18$$

Systems of Equations

You may be asked to solve for x and y in a **system of equations**, which is a group of related equations. You can often solve a simple system of equations using substitution. Look at this system of equations:

$$y = 2x$$
$$5x - y = 21$$

Substitute the value of y into the second equation:

$$5x - 2x = 21$$
$$3x = 21$$
$$x = \frac{21}{3}$$
$$x = 7$$

To find the value of y, substitute the value of x back into the original equation:

$$y = 2(x)$$
$$y = 2(7)$$
$$y = 14$$

Double-check your answer by substituting both answers into the second equation:

$$5(7) - 14 = 21$$
$$35 - 14 = 21$$

Now look at this system of equations:

$$x - 2y = 14$$
$$x + 3y = 9$$

Next eliminate one variable. You can eliminate x using subtraction:

$$x - 2y = 14$$
$$-x - 3y = -9$$
$$-5y = 5$$
$$y = -\frac{5}{5}$$
$$y = -1$$

To find the value of x, substitute the value of y into the original equation:

$$x - 2(-1) = 14$$
$$x + 2 = 14$$
$$x = 14 - 2$$
$$x = 12$$

Inequalities

An **inequality** compares two expressions by using one of the following signs:

>	greater than
<	less than
≥	greater than or equal to
≤	less than or equal to
≠	not equal to

Questions about inequalities might also use words such as *between, at least,* and *at most.*

Solving an inequality is very similar to solving an equation in that whatever you do to one side of an inequality, you must also do to the other. Look at this inequality:

$$3y > 21$$

Put y on a side by itself by dividing both sides by 3:

$$\frac{3y}{3} > \frac{21}{3}$$
$$y > 7,$$

which means that y can be any number that is greater than 7.

Note that one important difference between working with equations and working with inequalities is that if you divide or multiply both sides of an inequality by a negative number, you must *reverse* the inquality. For example, look at this inequality:

$$-3x \leq 15$$

To get x by itself on the left side of this inequality, you must divide by –3, and since that is a negative number, you must reverse the inequality. Therefore, you get

$$\frac{-3x}{-3} \geq \frac{15}{-3}, \text{ or}$$
$$x \geq -5.$$

You can check that this is correct by substituting various values for x. If you visualize the number line, you will remember that $x = -4$, for example, is greater than $x = -5$.

Let's Review 20: Equations and Expressions

Complete each of the following questions. Use the Tip below each question to help you choose the correct answer. When you finish, check your answers at the end of this chapter.

1. **A sporting goods store had 52 sweatshirts at the beginning of a sale. If *y* represents the number of sweatshirts sold during the sale, which expression shows the number of sweatshirts remaining?**

   A. $y - 52$

   B. $52(y)$

   C. $52 - y$

   D. $y + 52$

TIP

Remember that the store had 52 sweatshirts before the sale, so the amount sold would have to be subtracted from this amount.

2. **The number of plain white straws Cara has is shown by the expression $3x + 4$, with x representing her striped straws. If Cara has 10 striped straws, how many plain white straws does she have?**

   A. 16

   B. 30

   C. 34

   D. 70

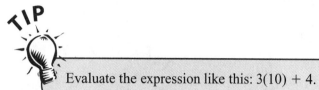

TIP

Evaluate the expression like this: $3(10) + 4$.

3. **Morgan's age is shown by the expression $a + 3$, where a represents Andrea's age. If Andrea is 9, how old is Morgan?**

   A. 6

   B. 9

   C. 12

   D. 15

TIP

Add 3 to Andrea's age.

4. **Solve for y, if $\frac{3}{y} = \frac{1}{2}$.**

   A. 2

   B. 3

   C. 4

   D. 6

TIP

What fraction with 3 as a numerator can be reduced to $\frac{1}{2}$?

5. A party planner charges a flat fee of $100 to plan a birthday party plus an additional $15 per guest. If n = the number of guests and c = total charges, which of the following shows how to determine the total charges?

A. $c = \$100 + \$15n$

B. $c = \$100n + 15$

C. $c = n + \dfrac{100}{15}$

D. $c = \dfrac{100n}{15}$

TIP

The flat fee is $100 no matter how many guests, and the variable is the number of guests.

6. The table below shows values for x and y for the equation $x^2 - y = 1$.

x	y
2	3
3	8
4	15
5	24
6	35
7	48
8	?

What value of y makes this equation true when $x = 8$?

A. 63

B. 64

C. 66

D. 68

TIP

Substitute 8 into the equation.

7. **A salesperson's total salary includes a base pay of $800 a month plus 2.5% of the monthly sales. If x = sales per month and y = total salary, which of the following shows how to determine the total salary for any month?**

   A. $\$800 = y + .025x$

   B. $y = \$800 + .025x$

   C. $y = 4800 \times .025x$

   D. $y = \$800x + .025$

TIP

Remember that 2.5% = .025, and 2.5% of the monthly sales amount will be added to the base pay.

8. **Given the inequality $3y < 18$, solve for y.**

   A. $y = 6$

   B. $y < 6$

   C. $y > 6$

   D. $y \le 6$

TIP

In this case, the sign in the answer should be the same as the sign in the original inequality.

Patterns

Patterns make it easy to predict what is next in a sequence. A pattern might be in the form of addition, subtraction, multiplication, or division of the same value for each number to get the next number, or it could be a combination of operations. Look at this problem:

What is the next number in this geometric sequence?

.04, 0.2, 1.0, 5.0, ___

You need to determine the pattern before you can find the next number. Look at the numbers. What is the difference between 1.0 and 5.0? It's 4, but this doesn't work for any of the other numbers. However, if you multiply 1.0 by 5 you get 5.0, and this also works for the other numbers. Therefore, the next number in the geometric sequence is $5.0(5) = 25.0$.

Linear Equations

A **linear equation** is an equation that forms a straight line when the values that are solutions to the equation are graphed. When you graph an equation, you substitute values for variables, which are unknown quantities. Linear equations usually have more than one variable. Look at the equation below:

$$x + y = 4$$

If you listed the numbers that could be substituted for the variables x and y, your list might look like this:

x	y
0	4
1	3
2	2
3	1
4	0

The x and y values are called **coordinates**. If you graphed these numbers and drew a line through the points, it would look like this:

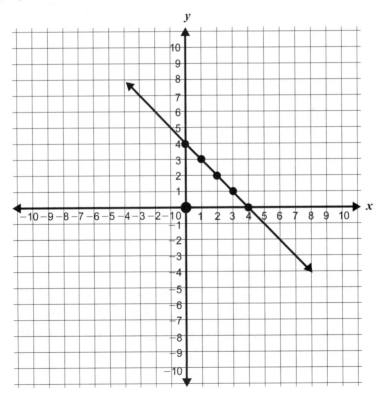

You may be asked to choose the correct graph of an equation, or you may be given a graph and asked to choose the correct equation. Either way, you can match a graph and equation if three or more coordinates are solutions for both. For the graph above, the points (0, 4), (1, 3), (2, 2), (3, 1), and (4, 0) are on the line, and they are also solutions to $x + y = 4$.

Functional Relationships

In very simple terms, a **function** is a relationship between two variables. A function takes some sort of *input,* usually a number, and changes it in some way to produce an *output*.

Look at the numbers in the table below.

x	y
1	5
2	6
3	7
4	8

The numbers in this table represent a function. Each pair of values is related in the same way ($y = x + 4$). For the values in this table, the coordinates are (1, 5), (2, 6), (3, 7), and (4, 8). To graph this function, you would plot these coordinates and then draw a line connecting them.

Not all coordinates represent a function, however. In a function, each value of x can correspond to only one value of y. For example, consider these coordinates: (2, 3), (2, −2). These coordinates cannot be part of a function because the x-coordinate, 2, has two y values, 3 and −2.

Vertical Line Test

When graphed, a function must pass the vertical line test. This means that a function will cross any vertical line (parallel to the *y*-axis) only once. The following graph represents a function:

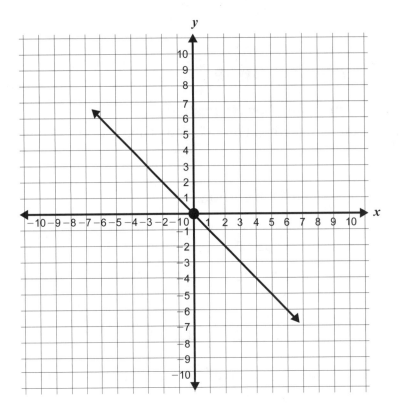

The next line does *not* represent a function because it crosses the *y*-axis more than once.

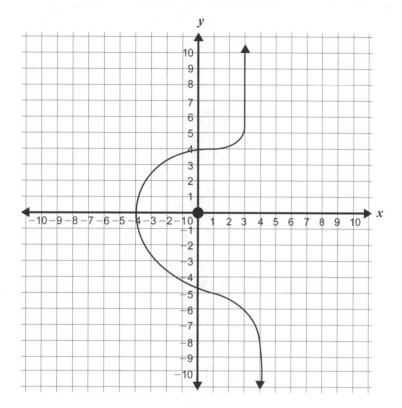

Linear Function

A **linear function** is a function that when graphed produces a straight line. A linear function is shown in the following graph:

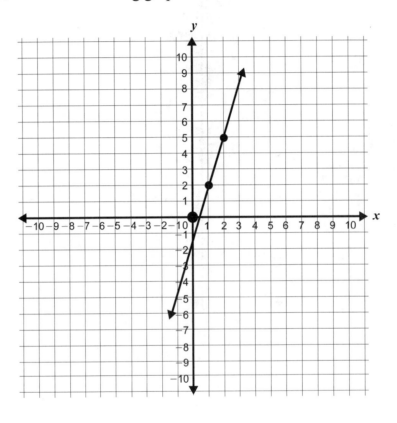

Let's Review 21: Linear Equations and Functional Relationships

Complete each of the following questions. Use the Tip below each question to help you choose the correct answer. When you finish, check your answers at the end of this chapter.

1. Nina is planning a party. The caterer she would like to hire charges $30 per guest and a set-up fee of $200. Nina has determined that the equation $y = 200 + 30x$ can be used to find the total cost of having this caterer cater the party based on the number of guests (x).

    For how many guests will Nina have paid the caterer exactly $3,200?

    A. 30

    B. 32

    C. 100

    D. 130

TIP

Substitute each of these numbers for x in the equation.

2.   **Which graph is not a function?**

A.

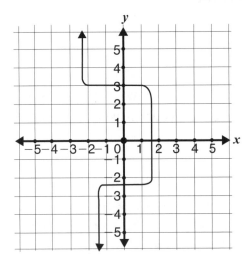

B.

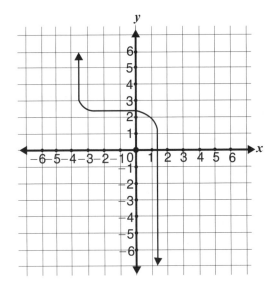

C.

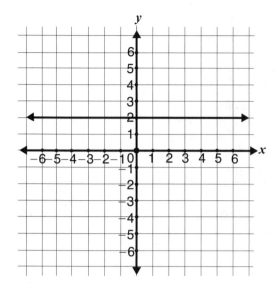

D.

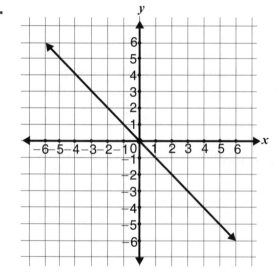

Remember the vertical line test.

3. **The number of children accepted into a summer reading program in Michelle's town is shown in the table below.**

Year	Number of Children
1	200
2	335
3	470
4	605

If this pattern continued, how many students would be accepted into the program in Year 5?

A. 705

B. 740

C. 755

D. 810

Find the difference between two consecutive years. See whether the same amount is added onto each year.

4. **Which graph represents a linear function?**

A.

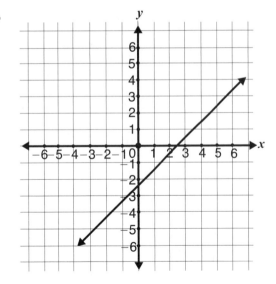

B.

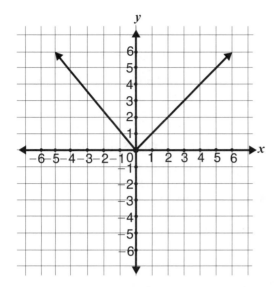

C.

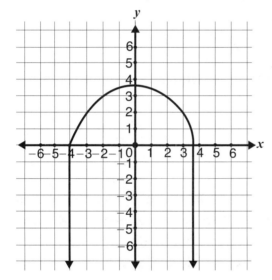

D.

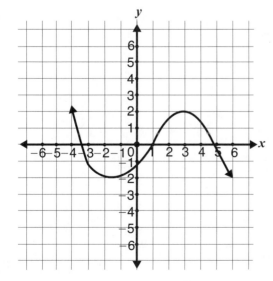

Inverse Relationships

An **inverse relationship** is one in which one variable increases as another decreases. For example, as a person's education increases, that person's chance of being unemployed decreases. Read this example:

Terri conducted research to see whether eating fruit decreases the number of colds a person gets in a year. She presented her findings in the table below.

Servings of Fruit	Number of Colds
0-1	9
2-3	8
3-4	5
5-6	2
7-8	1 or none

Terry's research shows an inverse relationship in which the more servings of fruit a person eats, the fewer colds that person gets.

Rate of Change

The **rate of change** of a function refers to the amount the function's output increases or decreases for each unit of change in the input. In other words, it is the difference between two x-coordinates and their corresponding y-coordinates. You can find the rate of change using this formula, in which d represents **differential**, a line's steepness:

$$\frac{dy}{dx}$$

Look at this graph:

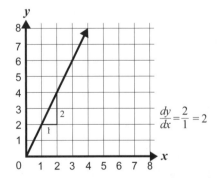

$$\frac{dy}{dx} = \frac{2}{1} = 2$$

The horizontal line shows the distance between two points along the *x*-axis and the vertical line shows the distance between two points along the *y*-axis. The rate of change for this line is 2.

Let's Review 22: Rate of Change

Complete each of the following questions. Use the Tip below each question to help you choose the correct answer. When you finish, check your answers at the end of this chapter.

1. **Which of the following describes the rate of change of the line below?**

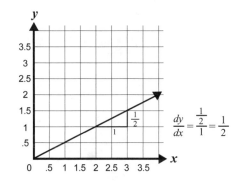

$$\frac{dy}{dx} = \frac{\frac{1}{2}}{1} = \frac{1}{2}$$

A. 0

B. $\dfrac{1}{2}$

C. 1

D. $\dfrac{11}{2}$

TIP

Substitute the differential for both the *x*- and *y*-axis.

2. **What is the slope of the line shown below?**

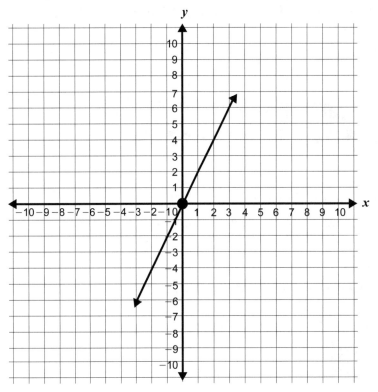

A. 0

B. $\frac{1}{2}$

C. 1

D. 2

TIP

Find the coordinates of two points on the line. Then use the rise-over-run formula.

Quadratic Functions

A **quadratic function** is a polynomial equation. This means it can have more than one term, in which the variable, usually x, is raised to the second power (squared) but not any higher than the second power.

Quadratic functions are functions in the form of

$$f(x) = ax^2 + bx + c$$

where a, b, and c are real numbers, and the coefficient a is not equal to zero. The notation $f(x)$ means "function of x." The following are quadratic functions:

$$f(x) = x^2 + 3x + 2$$
$$f(x) = 2x^2 + x - 1$$
$$f(x) = x^2 - 4x$$
$$f(x) = 4x^2 - 1$$

When graphed, quadratic functions produce a **parabola**, a curve that looks like the letter U, either right side up or upside down. While parabolas can vary in width, they all have this same basic shape.

The curve in the following graph is a parabola:

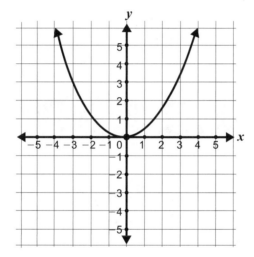

The path of a ball when it is thrown traces a parabola. The parabola begins when the ball is thrown. It reaches its highest point, its vertex, right before gravity starts to pull it downward. If the ball continues to bounce after it hits the ground, other parabolas are formed. Note that if a parabola faces downward, the vertex is the highest point.

You might be asked a question about changing the width of a parabola or moving a parabola up or down on the coordinate grid. The following are some general rules about parabolas of the form $f(x) = ax^2 + bx + c$:

- Positive values of coefficient a cause the parabola to open upward.

- Negative values of coefficient a cause the parabola to open downward.

- A negative c drops the parabola below the x-axis.

- As c increases, the vertex of the parabola gets higher.

- The greater the value of the coefficient a, the narrower the parabola.

Quadratic Equations

A **quadratic equation** is formed when a quadratic function is set equal to 0.

The equation below is a quadratic equation:

$$x^2 + 7x + 12 = 0$$

You may be asked to choose an equation that is equivalent to a given quadratic equation. For example, this equation is equivalent to the equation above:

$$(x + 3)(x + 4) = 0$$

Let's Review 23: Quadratic Equations

Complete each of the following questions. Use the Tip below each question to help you choose the correct answer. When you finish, check your answers with those in the Answer Key at the end of this chapter.

1. Which of the following is a graph of a quadratic equation?

A.

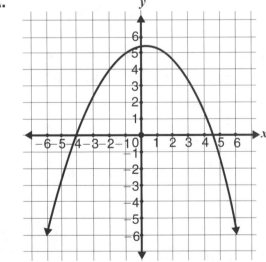

B.

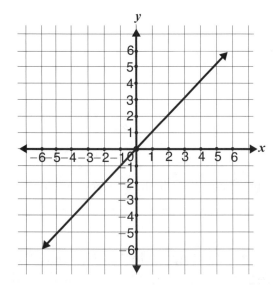

C.

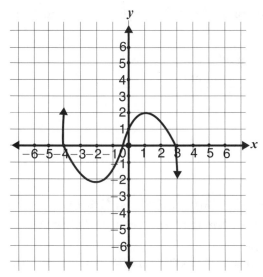

D.

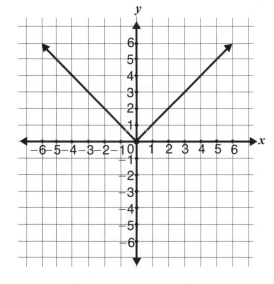

2. **Which equation is equivalent to**

   $x^2 + 7x - 2x - 14 = 0$?

   A. $(x - 7)(x + 2) = 0$

   B. $(x - 2)(x + 7) = 0$

   C. $(x - 2)(x - 14) = 0$

   D. $(x + 2)(x - 14) = 0$

TIP

Multiply the equations in the answer choices.

3. **For a patient on a weight-loss diet, a doctor kept a log of the number of hours per day his patient exercised for a month, and the number of pounds she lost each month. He recorded his findings in the table below.**

Hours per Day of Exercise	Patient's Weight Loss (pounds)
0.5	5
1	10
1.5	15
2	20

Which statement describes the relationship between the number of daily hours exercised and weight loss for this particular patient?

A. For a period of a month, an extra daily hour of exercise results in a loss of 5 pounds.

B. For a period of a month, an extra daily hour of exercise results in a loss of 10 pounds.

C. For a period of a month, an extra daily hour of exercise results in a loss of 15 pounds.

D. For a period of a month, an extra daily hour of exercise results in a loss of 20 pounds.

TIP

How many pounds did she lose when she exercised for one hour?

Chapter 8 Practice Problems

Complete each of the following practice problems. Check your answers at the end of this chapter. Be sure to read the answer explanations!

1. **A real estate agent is paid each time she sells a house. She is paid a flat fee of $1,000 and 4% of the sale price of the house. If s = sale price of the house and c = total payment, which of the following equations shows how to determine the real estate agent's payment?**

A. $c = \$1,000 + .004s$

B. $c = \$1,000 - .004s$

C. $c = \$1,000 + .04s$

D. $c = \$1,000 - .04s$

2. **Which graph represents the equation $y = x + 3$?**

A.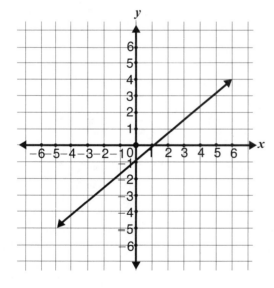

B.

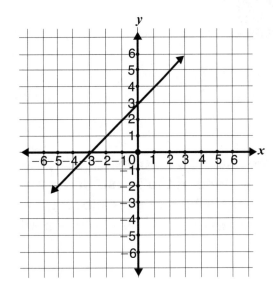

C.

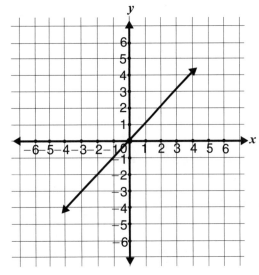

D.

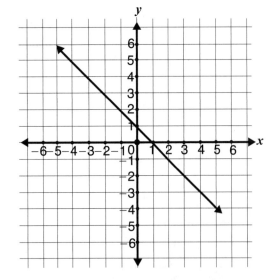

3. The number of cats at an animal shelter is shown by the expression $2y - 5$, with y representing the number of dogs. If the shelter has 125 dogs, how many cats does it have?

A. 130

B. 245

C. 250

D. 255

4. On the grid below, draw a graph representing the equation $y = x^2$?

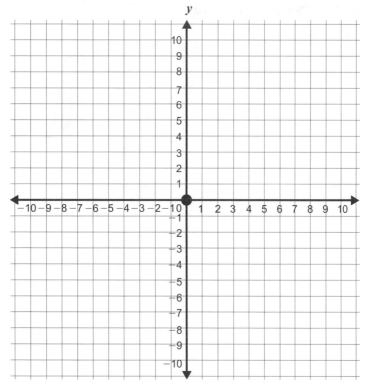

Explain whether or not this is a function. Why or why not? (2 points)

5. At a flea market, a vendor sold 1 handmade quilt and 2 antique plates for less than $100. If *q* represents the selling price of the quilt and *p* represents the selling price of one plate, which inequality could be used to show the amount of money the vendor made?

A. $q + p > \$100$

B. $q + 2p < \$100$

C. $q + p \geq \$100$

D. $q + 2p \geq \$100$

6. Which equation is equivalent to

$y^2 - 5y + 20y - 100 = 0$?

A. $(y - 20)(y + 5) = 0$

B. $(y + 20)(y - 5) = 0$

C. $(y + 10)(y - 15) = 0$

D. $(y - 4)(y + 5) = 0$

Chapter 8 Answer Explanations

Let's Review 20: Equations and Expressions

1. C

If the store had 52 sweatshirts before the sale and y represents the unknown number of sweatshirts sold during the sale, an expression that could be used to find the number of sweatshirts remaining is $52 - y$.

2. C

To evaluate the expression $3x + 4$, put 10 in place of x and simplify: $3(10) + 4 = 34$. Cara has 34 plain white straws.

3. C

If Andrea is 9 and Morgan is Andrea's age plus 3, Morgan is 12.

4. D

The fraction $\frac{3}{6}$ can be reduced to $\frac{1}{2}$. Another way to solve this equation is by cross-multiplication, which gives $3(2) = y(1)$, or $y = 6$.

5. A

In this case, the number of guests, n, is the variable, along with the cost, c. The cost is $15 times n plus the $100 flat fee. Answer choice A is correct.

6. A

If you substitute 8 for x in the equation, $x^2 - y = 1$, you get $8^2 - y = 1$. The correct answer is 63.

7. B

There are two variables in this equation, the salesperson's total salary and the monthly sales. The monthly sales should be multiplied by 2.5%, the percentage the salesperson will make on the total sales for the month, and this amount should be added to the base pay.

8. B

To solve this inequality, put y on one side by itself by dividing both sides by 3:

$$\frac{3y}{3} < \frac{18}{3}, \text{ or } y < 6$$

Let's Review 21: Linear Equations and Functional Relationships

1. C

If you substitute 100 into the equation for x, $y = 200 + 30(100)$, you get $3,200.

2. A

The first graph crosses the y-axis two times, so it is not a function.

3. B

To find the answer, add 135 to 605. 135 is the difference between the number of children from year 1 to 2, 2 to 3, and 3 to 4.

4. A

A linear function is a straight line. Answer choice A is the only answer option that is a straight line.

Let's Review 22: Rate of Change

1. B

If you substitute ½ and 1 into the formula *dy/dx* it will look like this: $\frac{1/2}{1} = \frac{1}{2}$.

2. D

If you substitute a pair of coordinates into the rise over run formula, such as $(-1, -2)$ and $(1, 2)$, you'll see that the slope is 2.

Let's Review 23: Quadratic Equations

1. A

A quadratic equation graphs as a parabola. Answer choice A is the correct answer.

2. B

If you multiply out $(x - 2)(x + 7) = 0$, you get the quadratic equation.

3. B

For a period of a month, an extra daily hour of exercise results in a loss of 10 pounds.

Chapter 8 Practice Problems

1. C

The percentage, .04, is multiplied by the sales price of the house, and this is added to the flat fee. Answer choice C is correct.

2. B

If you substitute numbers for *x* and plot them on the graph, you'll see that the second graph is correct.

3. B
To solve this expression, substitute the number of dogs for y in the expression $2y - 5$.

$2(125) - 5$, or 245.

4. Sample answer:

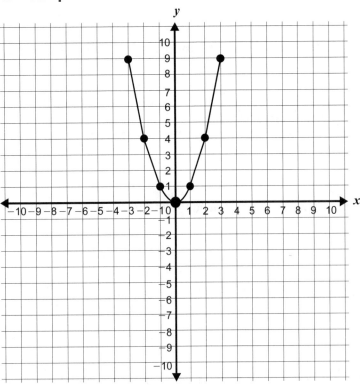

The graph is a function because it passes the vertical line test.

5. B
There are two plates, so you need to put the number 2 in front of p, the variable representing plates. He received less than \$100, so answer choice B is correct.

6. B
If you multiply out the equation in answer choice B, you'll see that it is equivalent to the quadratic equation.

OGT Mathematics
Practice Test

Directions: This Practice Test contains 44 questions.

Mark noted answers in the Answer Document section at the back of this book.

OGT Mathematics Reference Sheet

Information that may be needed to solve problems on the Mathematics Test:

Area Formulas

Parallelogram	$A = bh$
Rectangle	$A = lw$
Trapezoid	$A = \frac{1}{2}h(b_1 + b_2)$
Triangle	$A = \frac{1}{2}bh$

Circle Formulas

$$C = 2\pi r$$

$$\pi \approx 3.14 \text{ or } \frac{22}{7}$$

$$A = \pi r^2$$

Combinations

$$_nC_r = C(n,r) = \frac{n!}{r!(n-r)!}$$

Permutations

$$_nP_r = P(n,r) = \frac{n!}{(n-r)!}$$

Distance Formula

$$d = \sqrt{(x_2 - x_1)^2 + (y_2 - y_1)^2}$$

Quadratic Formula

$$x = \frac{-b \pm \sqrt{b^2 - 4ac}}{2a}$$

Volume Formulas

Cone	$V = \frac{1}{3}\pi r^2 h$	
Cylinder	$V = \pi r^2 h$	
Pyramid	$V = \frac{1}{3}Bh$	B = area of base
Rectangular Prism	$V = lwh$	
Right Prism	$V = Bh$	B = area of base
Sphere	$V = \frac{4}{3}\pi r^3$	

Trigonometry

$$\sin A = \frac{opposite}{hypotenuse}$$

$$\cos A = \frac{adjacent}{hypotenuse}$$

$$\tan A = \frac{opposite}{adjacent}$$

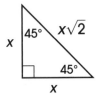

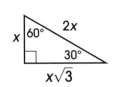

PRACTICE TEST 1

Directions: For multiple-choice items, choose the best answer and then fill in the corresponding space on your Answer Document. If you change an answer, be sure to erase the first mark completely. When you respond to the short-answer and extended-response items, you do not have to use the entire area of the space provided. The use of the grid paper on your Answer Document is optional unless otherwise stated. Be sure that your answers are complete and all your work appears on the Answer Document.

---

1. In $\triangle ABC$ below, $\angle B$ is a right angle.

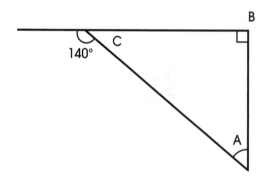

For question 1, respond completely on your **Answer Document**. (2 points)

On your **Answer Document**, determine the measure of $\angle A$. Explain in words how you determined the measure of $\angle A$.

2. In a card game, Andy scored 22, 5, 22, 13, 12, 24, 24, 9, 20, and 19 points. What is the mean number of points Andy scored?

   A. 17

   B. 18

   C. 19

   D. 24

3. The measurements, in centimeters, of the sides of a right triangle are shown below.

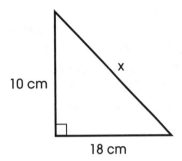

10 cm

x

18 cm

What number is closest to the length of the hypotenuse of this right triangle?

A. 12 cm

B. 16 cm

C. 21 cm

D. 24 cm

4. Shamus earns $10.00 an hour at his summer job. His employer must pay him "time and a half" ($1\frac{1}{2}$ times his regular hourly earnings) for each hour over 40 hours per week. His employer withholds 16% of his gross pay for various taxes. The table below shows Shamus's work time for the week.

For question 4, respond completely on your **Answer Document.** (2 points)

Shamus's Hours

Mon	Tue	Wed	Thu	Fri
$8\frac{1}{2}$ h	10 h	$9\frac{3}{4}$ h	$8\frac{1}{4}$ h	9 h

On your **Answer Document**, determine the amount of Shamus's paycheck, after taxes are withheld, for the week shown in the table. Show your work or provide an explanation to support your answer.

Go to next page

5. An author of a novel is paid by the publisher for the rights to publish his book. The author is paid $5,000 plus 6% of the book sales. If s = book sales and c = total payment, which of the following equations shows how to determine the total payment?

A. $c = \$5,000 + .006s$

B. $c = \$5,000 - .006s$

C. $c = \$5,000 + .06s$

D. $c = \$5,000 - .06s$

6. Which equation is equivalent to $2(3y - 5) = 4(y + 2)$?

A. $2y = 18$

B. $10y = 18$

C. $10y = -18$

D. $2y = -18$

7. The results of a survey asking how students get to school are shown below.

Bus	58%
Drive	22%
Walk	10%
Other	10%

Which type of graph should be used to show the results of the survey?

A. bar graph

B. circle graph

C. pictograph

D. line graph

8. Use the data in the following chart to determine the median number of students in a grade.

Number of Students in Emma's School

Grade	Number of Students
1	20
2	28
3	27
4	22
5	25
6	26
7	27

A. 20

B. 22

C. 25

D. 26

Go to next page

9. Kayla needs to make a cube for a school
   project. She plans to cut a shape out of thick
   cardboard and then fold it to make a cube.
   Which of these nets or shapes could Kayla use
   to make her model?

A.

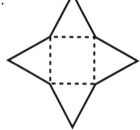

B.

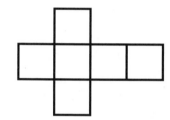

C.

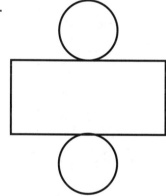

D.

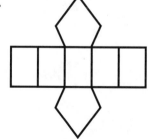

10. Triangle ABC has vertices at the coordinates (−5, 1), (−7, 5), and (−3, 5), as shown.

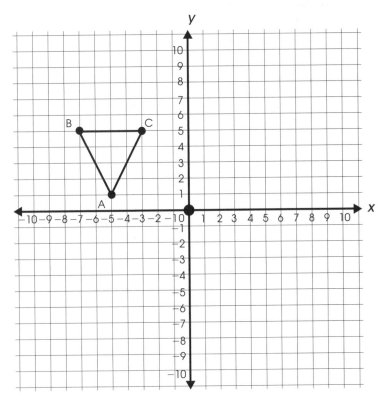

What are the coordinates of the vertices of triangle ABC when it is reflected over the x-axis?

A. (7, 5), (3, 5), (5, 9)

B. (−5, −1), (−7, −5), (−3, −5)

C. (5, 1), (3, 5), (7, 5)

D. (5, −1), (7, −5), (3, −5)

11. The mass of a dust particle is 0.00000000075 gram. What is this number in scientific notation?

    A. 7.5×10^{10}

    B. 7.5×10^{-10}

    C. 7.5×10^{9}

    D. 7.5×10^{-9}

12. What is the area of a circle with a radius of 8 centimeters?

    A. 25 square centimeters

    B. 50 square centimeters

    C. 201 square centimeters

    D. 402 square centimeters

13. Which of the following numbers is irrational?

    A. -9

    B. $\dfrac{49}{7}$

    C. 3

    D. $\sqrt{10}$

Go to next page

14. A school had 38 cheerleading uniforms at the beginning of the school year. If *x* represents the number of additional cheerleading uniforms purchased during the school year, which expression shows the number of cheerleading uniforms at the end of the school year?

    A. $\dfrac{38}{x}$

    B. 38 – *x*

    C. 32(*x*)

    D. 38 + *x*

15. Leeann wants to conduct a survey to determine the disc jockey the students want at their semi-formal.

Which sample population should Leeann survey to represent the entire student body?

    A. randomly survey students in the cafeteria

    B. survey three students on a bus to school

    C. randomly survey the teachers

    D. survey students in the chess club

Go to next page

16. If the mean number of people who visited a museum over 5 days is 250, what is the total attendance during the 5 days?

    A. 750

    B. 1,000

    C. 1,250

    D. 2,500

17. At the end of the marking period, Devon earned 428 points out of a possible 500 points, and Manuel earned 450 points out of a possible 500 points.

    On your Answer Document, determine how much greater the percentage of Manuel's points are than Devon's.

For question 17, respond completely on your **Answer Document**. (2 points)

Go to next page

18. Which graph represents the equation $y = x + 2$?

A.

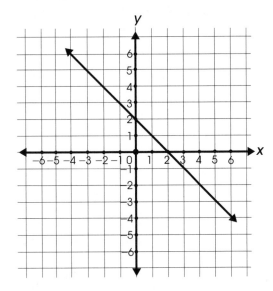

B.

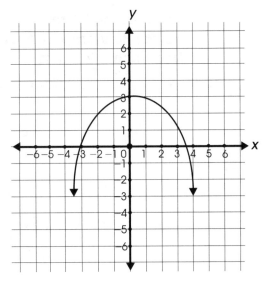

C.

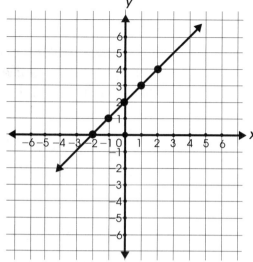

D.

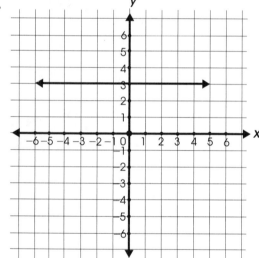

Go to next page

19. Ray has decided to enter a local marathon. As part of his training, he is going to increase the number of miles he rides his bike every week by 5 miles.

    On your Answer Document, determine how many miles Ray will ride in the fifth week if he rides 35 miles in the first week.

For question 19, respond completely on your **Answer Document**. (2 points)

20. Which is the slope of a line that passes through the points (2, 2) and (−3, −3)?

    A. 1

    B. −1

    C. 2

    D. −2

21. What is 34,000 expressed in scientific notation?

    A. 3.4×10^2

    B. 3.4×10^3

    C. 3.4×10^4

    D. 34×10^3

22. Find the missing length (x) of the pair of similar figures shown below.

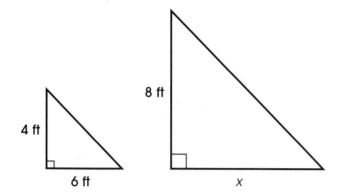

A. 8 feet

B. 10 feet

C. 12 feet

D. 18 feet

23. Tamara conducted an experiment and recorded the data in the table shown below. Which equation did she use to solve for values of y?

x	y
1	−1
2	2
3	7
4	14

A. $y = x^2 - 2$

B. $y = x^2$

C. $y = x^2 - 1$

D. $y = x - 3$

24. Renee needs to simplify the following expression for her homework assignment.

$$3(2x - y) + 4(2x + y) + 3(x + y)$$

Which of the following expressions is equivalent to the expression above?

A. $17x + 4y$

B. $3x + 4y$

C. $17x + 14y$

D. $14x - 4y$

25. Find the probability of spinning "blue" on the spinner below.

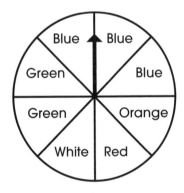

A. $\frac{1}{8}$

B. $\frac{1}{4}$

C. $\frac{3}{8}$

D. $\frac{1}{2}$

26. What is the volume of the box pictured below?

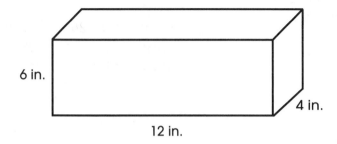

6 in.

4 in.

12 in.

   A. 22 cubic inches

   B. 72 cubic inches

   C. 288 cubic inches

   D. 576 cubic inches

27. The perimeter of a triangle is 28. Two of its sides measure 10 and 8. What is the length of the remaining side?

   A. 6

   B. 8

   C. 10

   D. 12

Go to next page

28. A contractor uses a 15-foot ladder to reach the roof. The ladder is 9 feet away from the house. The ladder, house, and ground form a right triangle.

For question 28, respond completely on your **Answer Document**. (4 points)

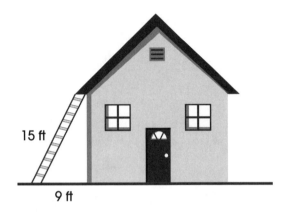

15 ft

9 ft

On your **Answer Document**, find how far up the house the ladder will reach. Then determine the area of the triangle.

29. A school has a budget of $100,000 for building improvements. It needs a new roof (*x*) and an addition (*y*). Which of the following inequalities represents how much the school can spend?

A. $x + y > \$100,000$

B. $x + y < \$100,000$

C. $x + y \geq \$100,000$

D. $x + y \leq \$100,000$

Go to next page

30. The graph below shows the estimated number of manatees counted in Florida from 1995 to 2006.

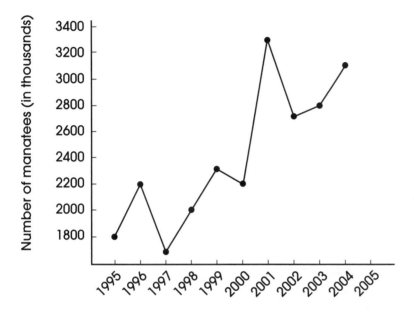

The Manatee Population in Florida

If the manatee population continues to increase at the same rate as that shown between the years 2003 and 2004, which of the following gives the best estimate of the number of manatees in Florida in the year 2005?

A. 1 to 2 thousand

B. 2 to 3 thousand

C. 3 to 4 thousand

D. 4 to 5 thousand

Go to next page

31. In Casey's town, 1 out of 5 people are over the age of 70. Her town has an estimated population of 120,000. Based on this information, approximately how many people in Casey's town are over the age of 70?

    A. 24,000

    B. 30,000

    C. 60,000

    D. 600,000

32. The number of students enrolled in introductory courses at a university is shown on the graph below. How many more students are enrolled in Composition than in Psychology?

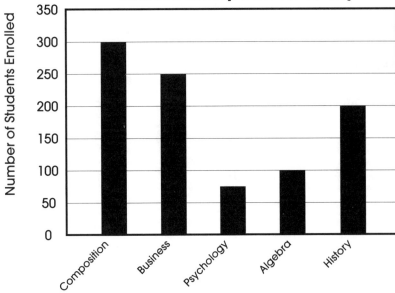

College Enrollment in Introductory Courses at Anytown University

    A. 200

    B. 225

    C. 250

    D. 375

33. Emily works in a small crafts store where the cash register does not compute the sales tax. If the sales tax is 6%, what amount should Emily add to a purchase of $12.00?

    A. $0.60

    B. $0.72

    C. $6.00

    D. $7.20

34. There are 20 straws in a box; some are red and some are blue. The probability of reaching into the box without looking and pulling out a red straw is $\frac{3}{5}$. How many blue straws are in the box?

    A. 3

    B. 6

    C. 8

    D. 12

Go to next page

35. Look at the similar triangles shown below.

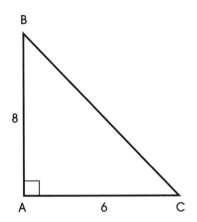
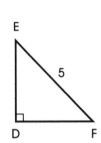

For question 35, respond completely on your **Answer Document**. (4 points)

On your Answer Document, explain in geometric terms what is meant by "△ABC is similar to △DEF." Determine the length of the hypotenuse in △ABC. Find the length of line ED and DF in △DEF.

36. Solve for x, if 2x = 16.

   A. 6

   B. 7

   C. 8

   D. 9

37. Which of the numbers below is the greatest?

   A. $\sqrt{132}$

   B. 1.32×10^2

   C. 12% of 132

   D. $\dfrac{132}{12}$

38. Look at line *a* in the graph below.

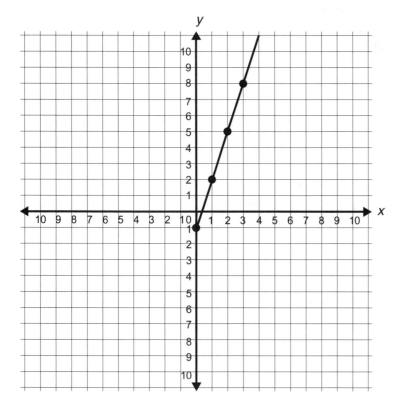

What is the slope of this line?

A. 0

B. $\frac{5}{2}$

C. $\frac{1}{3}$

D. 3

39. Kaitlyn has $80 to go shopping. She wants to buy a jacket priced at *a* dollars and a pair of shoes priced at *b* dollars. Which inequality shows how much Kaitlyn can spend?

   A. $a + b = \$80$

   B. $a + b \leq \$80$

   C. $a + b < \$80$

   D. $a + b \geq \$80$

40. Figure *ABCD* is an isosceles trapezoid.

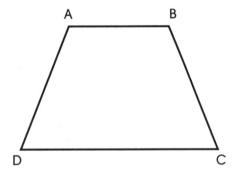

   Which of the following statements about trapezoids is true?

   A. Lines *AB* and *CD* are parallel.

   B. Lines *BC* and *AD* are perpendicular.

   C. $\angle A$ and $\angle C$ are congruent.

   D. $\angle A$ and $\angle D$ are congruent.

41. A high-speed train travels 500 miles an hour. How far will it travel in $3\frac{1}{2}$ hours?

    A. 1,500 miles

    B. 1,625 miles

    C. 1,750 miles

    D. 2,000 miles

42. Figure *ABCDEFGH* is a regular octagon.

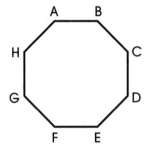

    What is the measure, in degrees, of $\angle FGH$?

    A. 108°

    B. 120°

    C. 135°

    D. 180°

Stop

43. Which equation is equivalent to
$3(3x + 2) = 4(x + 2)$?

   A. $13x = 14$

   B. $13x = -14$

   C. $5x = 2$

   D. $5x = -2$

44. Which expression represents 63,000 written in scientific notation?

   A. $.63 \times 10^5$

   B. 6.3×10^4

   C. 63×10^3

   D. 630×10^2

Practice Test 1 Answer Explanations

1. (Measurement: D)
Sample answer: The angle labeled $140°$ is supplementary to $\angle C$ in the triangle. This means that the measure of the two angles is $180°$. Therefore, $\angle C$ is $40°$. We know that the measure of $\angle B$ is $90°$ because it is a right angle. The sum of the angles in a triangle is $180°$. The sum of $\angle B$ and $\angle C$ is $130°$. Therefore, the measure of $\angle A$ must be $50°$.

2. A (Data Analysis and Probability: C)
To find the mean number of points Andy scored, total his points (170). Then divide by 10. The answer is 17.

3. C (Measurement: D)
Use the Pythagorean Theorem to find the length of the hypotenuse:
$10^2 + 18^2 = 100 + 324 = 424$; $c^2 = 424$; $c = \sqrt{424} \approx 21$cm.

4. (Measurement: F)
Sample answer: Shamus's hours total 45.5. His regular pay for the first 40 hours is $400.00. His hourly overtime rate is $15.00 an hour. He worked 5.5 hours of overtime, so $15 \times 5.5 = \$82.50$. His weekly salary plus his overtime is therefore $482.50. The amount of money withheld for taxes is $\$482.50 \times .16 = \$77.20$. Therefore, his paycheck is $\$482.50 - \$77.20 = \$405.30$.

5. C (Algebra: H)
If the author is paid a flat fee of $5,000 to publish the book, plus 6% (.06) sales, the number of books sold is the variable. Therefore, the best equation is $c = \$5,000 + .06s$.

6. A (Patterns, Functions, and Algebra: D)
If you multiply out the equation, you get $6y - 10 = 4y + 8$; then combine like terms: $2y = 18$.

7. B (Data Analysis and Probability: B)
A circle graph is the best kind of graph to display percentages.

8. D (Data Analysis and Probability: C)
To find the median number of students, put the number of students in each grade in order from least to greatest. The number in the middle, in this case 26, is the median.

9. B **(Geometry and Spatial Sense: E)**

The net in answer choice B is the only one that has six faces that are all squares.

10. B **(Geometry and Spatial Sense: D)**

Remember that a reflection is a mirror image. Therefore, when the triangle is reflected over the *x*-axis, it will look as if it's upside-down.

11. B **(Number Sense: A)**

To write 0.00000000075 gram in scientific notation, you need to move the decimal point so that it is between 7 and 5. In this case, you need to move it 10 places. You're moving the decimal point to the right, so the exponent of 10 is negative.

12. C **(Measurement: C)**

If you use the formula $A = \pi r^2$, you'll see that the area is 201 square centimeters.

13. D **(Number Sense: D)**

An irrational number cannot be expressed as a fraction. It is non-ending and non-repeating. Therefore, $\sqrt{10}$ is irrational.

14. D **(Patterns, Functions, and Algebra: D)**

If the school began the year with 38 cheerleading uniforms and then purchased more (*x*), the correct expression is $38 + x$.

15. A **(Data Analysis and Probability: G)**

The only survey without bias is answer choice A, to survey the students in the cafeteria. Surveying three students on a bus to school (answer choice B) is not enough to get an idea what disc jockey all of the students want. Surveying the teachers (answer choice C) won't give you an idea of the student's opinions, and the students in the chess club (answer choice D) might share similar interests that are not representative of all of the students.

16. C **(Data Analysis and Probability: D)**

To find out how many people attended the museum over five days, multiply the mean by 5, which is 1,250.

17. (Number Sense: G)

Sample answer: To solve this problem, you need to find the percentage of Devon's points and the percentage of Manuel's points:

Devon's points: $\frac{428}{500} = .856 \times 100 =$ about 86%

Manuel's points: $\frac{450}{500} = .9 \times 100 = 90\%$

Then you need to find the difference between these percentages:

$90\% - 86\% = 4\%$

18. C   (Geometry and Spatial Sense: D)

If you substitute numbers for x in the equation $y = x + 2$, and then plot the coordinates for x and y, you'll see that answer choice C is correct.

19. (Patterns, Functions, and Algebra: J)

Sample answer: If Ray rides his bike 35 miles the first week and plans to increase his number of miles by 5 miles a week, in the second week he will ride 40 miles, and he will ride 55 miles by the fifth week.

20. A   (Geometry and Spatial Sense: D)

To find the slope of the line, use this formula: $\frac{(y_2 - y_1)}{(x_2 - x_1)}$, or $\frac{(-3 - 2)}{(-3 - 2)}$. The answer is $\frac{-5}{-5}$ or 1.

21. C   (Number Sense: A)

With scientific notation, you move the decimal point until it is between the 3 and 4. The number of places is the exponent of 10, and because you are moving it to the left, the exponent is positive.

22. C   (Measurement: D)

The measurements of the second triangle are double the first, so the base of the second triangle is 12 feet.

23. A   (Algebra: E)

Plug values into each formula to choose the correct one. If you plug the values 1, 2, 3, 4 for x in the formula in answer choice A, you'll see that this answer choice is correct.

24. A   (Patterns, Functions, and Algebra: D)

The expression can be simplified like this:

$6x - 3y + 8x + 4y + 3x + 3y = 17x + 4y$

25. C **(Data Analysis and Probability: J)**

There are eight sections of the spinner, so this is the denominator. Three sections are blue, so the probability of spinning blue is $\frac{3}{8}$.

26. C **(Measurement: C)**

$A = lwh$. If you multiply 12 by 6 and then that answer by 4, you get 288.

27. C **(Measurement: C)**

Add the lengths of the two sides that are provided and then subtract this sum from the perimeter: $10 + 8 = 18$; $28 - 18 = 10$.

28. (Measurement: D)

Use the Pythagorean Theorem, $a^2 + b^2 = c^2$, where c is the length of the ladder (hypotenuse in the figure). Then

$$9^2 + b^2 = 15^2$$
$$b^2 = 15^2 - 9^2$$
$$b^2 = 225 - 81$$
$$b^2 = 144$$
$$\sqrt{b^2} = \sqrt{144}$$
$$b = 12$$

The ladder will reach 12 feet up on the house. To find the area of this triangle, use the formula:

$$A = \frac{1}{2}bh$$
$$A = \frac{1}{2}(9 \times 12)$$
$$A = \frac{1}{2}(108)$$

$A = 54$ square feet

29. D **(Patterns, Functions, and Algebra: D)**

The inequality should be "less than or equal to" since the school can't go over $100,000, but it can spend this exact amount.

30. C   **(Data Analysis and Probability: A)**

If the manatee population continued to increase at about the same rate, there would be between three and four thousand manatees in 2005.

31. A   **(Number Sense: G)**

To answer this problem, set up a ratio as $\frac{1}{5} = \frac{x}{120,000}$. Cross multiply to get $5x = 120,000$, or $x = 24,000$.

32. B   **(Data Analysis and Probability: A)**

About 300 students are enrolled in composition and 75 are enrolled in psychology. If you subtract 75 from 300, the answer is 225.

33. B   **(Number Sense: G)**

$6\% = .06$. To find the amount of tax Emily needs to add, multiply $12 by $.06$. The answer is $0.72.

34. C   **(Data Analysis and Probability: I)**

Since there are 20 straws in the box, and $\frac{3}{5}$ are red, the number of red straws is $20 \times \frac{3}{5} = 12$. The number of blue straws would be equal to the total number of straws minus the number of red straws; $20 - 12 = 8$. So 8 straws must be blue.

35. (Measurement: D)

Sample answer: If two triangles are similar, their corresponding sides and areas have similar proportions.

$$a^2 + b^2 = c^2$$
$$8^2 + 6^2 = c^2$$
$$64 + 36 = 100$$
$$\sqrt{100} = 10$$
$$c = 10 = \text{hypotenuse}$$

For DE:

$$\frac{AB}{DE} = \frac{BC}{EF}, \text{ or}$$
$$\frac{8}{x} = \frac{10}{5}$$
$$10x = 40$$
$$x = DE = 4$$

For DF:

$$\frac{AC}{DF} = \frac{BC}{EF}, \text{ or}$$

$$\frac{6}{y} = \frac{10}{5}$$

$$10y = 30$$

$$y = DF = 3$$

36. C   (Patterns, Functions, and Algebra: D)

To solve this problem, put x on one side of the equation: $\frac{2x}{2} = \frac{16}{2}$, or $x = 8$.

37. B   (Data Analysis and Probability: E)

To solve this problem, determine the values for each answer choice. Answer choice A is 11.49. Answer choice B is 132. Answer choice C is 15.84, and answer choice D is 11. Therefore, answer choice B is the greatest.

38. D   (Geometry and Spatial Sense: D)

(2, 5) (3, 8) may be substituted into the equation:

$$\frac{y_2 - y_1}{x_2 - x_1}$$

$$\frac{8 - 5}{3 - 2}$$

The slope is 3.

39. B   (Patterns, Functions, and Algebra: D)

The sign in the inequality should be equal to or less than, since Kaitlyn can't spend more than $80.

40. A   (Geometry and Spatial Sense: A)

All trapezoids have exactly one pair of parallel sides. In an isoceles trapezoid, as we have here, the base angles are also congruent. But the base angles in this case are angles C and D, not angles A and D.

41. C   **(Patterns, Functions, and Algebra: J)**
To solve this problem, multiply 500 by 3.5. The answer is 1,750 miles.

42. C   **(Geometry and Spatial Sense: A)**
Each angle in a regular octagon measures 135°.

43. C   **(Patterns, Functions and Algebra: F)**
$3(3x + 2) = 4(x + 2)$

$9x + 6 = 4x + 8$ distribute the numbers in front of the parentheses to the terms inside
$9x = 4x + 2$ subtract 6 from each side of the equation
$5x = 2$ subtract $4x$ from each side of the equation

44. B   **(Number, Number Sense and Operations: A)**
Take the number 63,000 and move the decimal point to the left 4 places, which is 6. The number becomes 6.3 times 10 raised to the 4th power or 6.3×10^4.

OGT Mathematics
Practice Test

2

Directions: This Practice Test contains 44 questions.

Mark noted answers in the Answer Document section at the back of this book.

OGT Mathematics Reference Sheet

Information that may be needed to solve problems on the Mathematics Test:

Area Formulas

Parallelogram	$A = bh$
Rectangle	$A = lw$
Trapezoid	$A = \frac{1}{2}h(b_1 + b_2)$
Triangle	$A = \frac{1}{2}bh$

Circle Formulas

$$C = 2\pi r$$

$$\pi \approx 3.14 \text{ or } \frac{22}{7}$$

$$A = \pi r^2$$

Combinations

$$_nC_r = C(n,r) = \frac{n!}{r!(n-r)!}$$

Permutations

$$_nP_r = P(n,r) = \frac{n!}{(n-r)!}$$

Distance Formula

$$d = \sqrt{(x_2 - x_1)^2 + (y_2 - y_1)^2}$$

Quadratic Formula

$$x = \frac{-b \pm \sqrt{b^2 - 4ac}}{2a}$$

Volume Formulas

Cone	$V = \frac{1}{3}\pi r^2 h$	
Cylinder	$V = \pi r^2 h$	
Pyramid	$V = \frac{1}{3}Bh$	B = area of base
Rectangular Prism	$V = lwh$	
Right Prism	$V = Bh$	B = area of base
Sphere	$V = \frac{4}{3}\pi r^3$	

Trigonometry

$$\sin A = \frac{opposite}{hypotenuse}$$

$$\cos A = \frac{adjacent}{hypotenuse}$$

$$\tan A = \frac{opposite}{adjacent}$$

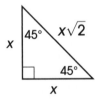
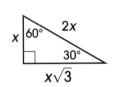

PRACTICE TEST 2

Directions: For multiple-choice items, choose the best answer and then fill in the corresponding space on your Answer Document. If you change an answer, be sure to erase the first mark completely. When you respond to the short-answer and extended-response items, you do not have to use the entire area of the space provided. The use of the grid paper on your Answer Document is optional unless otherwise stated. Be sure that your answers are complete and all your work appears in the Answer Document.

1. Frankie has 30 baseball cards at the beginning of the week. If x represents the number of baseball cards Frankie gave to his friend Amy on Tuesday and y represents the number of baseball cards his mother gave to him on Thursday, which expression shows the number of baseball cards Frankie has at the end of the week?

   A. $x + 30 - y$

   B. $30 - x + y$

   C. $30x - y$

   D. $30y + x$

Go to next page

2.   Find the probability of spinning a "2" on the spinner below.

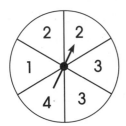

   A. $\frac{1}{16}$

   B. $\frac{1}{4}$

   C. $\frac{1}{3}$

   D. $\frac{1}{2}$

3.   Which number below is the greatest?

   A. $\sqrt{196}$

   B. $3\sqrt{12}$

   C. 2^4

   D. 3^3

4.   Jeffrey needs to simplify the following expression for his homework assignment.
     $4(x + 2y) + 2(3x - y) - (x + y)$

   Which of the following expressions is equivalent to the expression above?

   A. $9x - 7y$

   B. $9x + 7y$

   C. $9x - 5y$

   D. $9x + 5y$

5. Peter bought a mountain bike for $195.99. When he took the bike home, he noticed a large scratch on one side. Therefore, the bike shop gave Peter a 35% refund on the bike. What was the price of the bike after the discount was applied?

For question 5, respond completely on your **Answer Document**. (2 points)

6. The table shows the number of people in Renee's school who speak a language other than English.

Students Speaking a Language Other than English

German	18
Spanish	124
Arabic	25
Italian	3
French	34
Other	27

Which type of graph is appropriate to display this data?

A. bar graph

B. box-and-whiskers plot

C. line graph

D. scatterplot

Go to next page

7. The average salary for all restaurant workers in a certain area is $275 a week. The weekly salaries of seven employees at Lobster King are given in the table below.

For question 7, respond completely on your **Answer Document**. (4 points)

Employee 1	$200
Employee 2	$225
Employee 3	$240
Employee 4	$240
Employee 5	$280
Employee 6	$375
Employee 7	$400

In your **Answer Document**, determine the measures of central tendency (mean, median, and mode) of the seven salaries.

Specify which of these measures of center the management could use to represent the salaries in an argument against pay increases. Explain your answer.

Specify which of these measures of central tendency the labor union could use to represent the salaries in an argument for pay increases. Explain your answer. (4 points)

8. Patrick is selecting a menu for a party. He can choose from chicken, fish, or roast beef as a main dish. As a side dish, he can choose from salad, green beans, baked potatoes, mashed potatoes, or apple sauce. How many combinations of main dish and side dish can Patrick choose?

    A. 8

    B. 15

    C. 30

    D. 45

9. Lisa has a bag of 30 marbles. Five of these marbles are white, 3 are blue, 10 are pink, 5 are red, 2 are green, 3 are orange, and 2 are black. If Lisa reaches into the bag and pulls out a marble without looking, what is the probability that she will pull out a red marble?

    A. $\frac{1}{30}$

    B. $\frac{1}{6}$

    C. $\frac{1}{5}$

    D. $\frac{1}{4}$

Go to next page

10. The approximate value of $\sqrt{20}$ is labeled by a point on the number line.

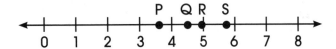

Which of the points correctly displays this value?

A. P

B. Q

C. R

D. S

11. A high school basketball court that meets regulation size requirements measures 94 feet long and 50 feet wide.

For question 11, respond completely on your **Answer Document**. (2 points)

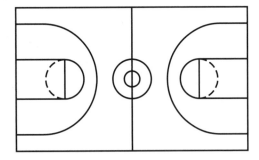

Leo's elementary school uses a basketball court that is similar in size and shape, but with a length 20 feet shorter than the high school regulation basketball court. In your **Answer Document**, determine the width, in feet, of the elementary school basketball court.
(2 points)

12. A can of soup has a diameter of 3 inches and a height of 4 inches.

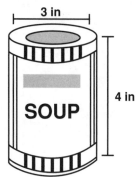

3 in

4 in

SOUP

For question 12, respond completely on your **Answer Document**. (2 points)

The company decided to increase either the diameter by 1 inch or the height by 1 inch. In your **Answer Document**, determine the difference, in cubic inches, in capacity obtained by increasing the diameter by 1 inch and the capacity obtained by increasing the height 1 inch. Show your computations on the two new capacities or give a complete explanation with numerical support to justify your answer. (4 points)

Go to next page

13. Three vertices of a quadrilateral are (1, 3), (6, 3), and (1, 6).

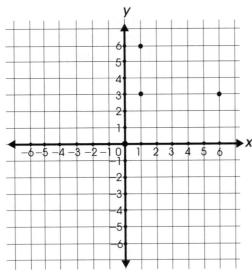

When used as the last vertex, which point would make the quadrilateral a rectangle?

A. (3, 6)

B. (5, 6)

C. (6, 6)

D. (7, 6)

14. Deanne is making a wallpaper border using the triangle shown below. Classify the triangle according to the lengths of its sides.

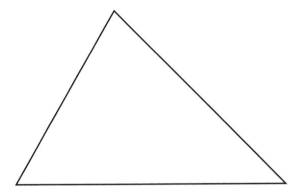

A. acute triangle

B. equilateral triangle

C. isosceles triangle

D. obtuse triangle

15. Which figure is not a parallelogram?

A.

B.

C.

D.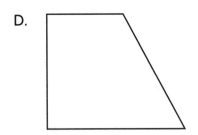

16. In 2006, 131 million people in the United States were employed. Of these, about 13% worked in manufacturing jobs.

    In your **Answer Document**, determine how many people in the United States were employed in manufacturing jobs in 2006. (2 points)

    For question 16, respond completely on your **Answer Document**. (2 points)

17. What is the volume of the box pictured below?

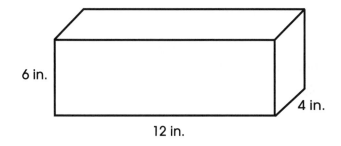

6 in.   12 in.   4 in.

A. 22 cubic inches

B. 72 cubic inches

C. 288 cubic inches

D. 576 cubic inches

18. Dawn recorded the number of cats adopted at her local animal shelter from January through July, as shown in the table below.

For question 18, respond completely on your **Answer Document**. (2 points)

Number of Cats Adopted

January	210
February	180
March	212
April	210
May	195
June	195
July	220

In your **Answer Document**, determine the mean number of cats adopted at the animal shelter. (2 points)

19. Melanie uses the expression $8a + 12b$ to determine the amount she earns at a pay rate of 8 dollars an hour plus time and a half for overtime. One week she worked 40 hours, plus 8 hours of overtime.

In your **Answer Document**, determine her total pay for the week. Show your work. (2 points)

For question 19, respond completely on your **Answer Document**. (2 points)

20. Which graph represents a linear function?

A.

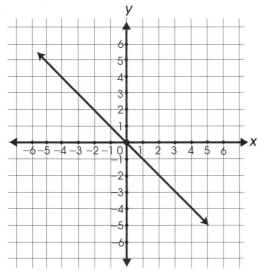

C.

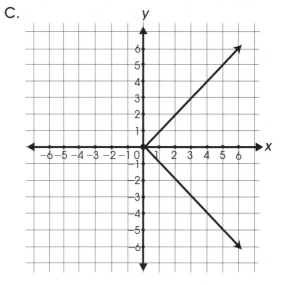

B.

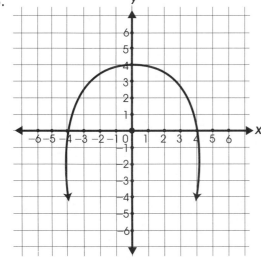

D.

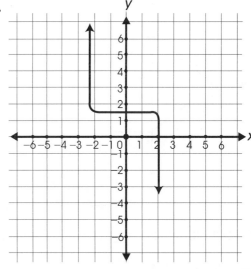

Go to next page

21. Charlie wants the mean of his five English test scores to be at least 85%. His scores on the first four tests are 80%, 83%, 90%, and 92%. What is the minimum score Charlie can earn on the fifth test to meet his goal?

    A. 75

    B. 80

    C. 85

    D. 90

22. The figure below shows a net for a 3-dimensional object.

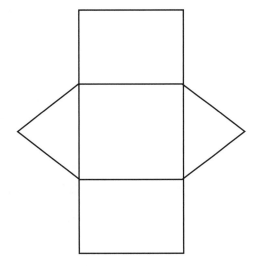

    When folded, which object will this net produce?

    A. triangular prism

    B. square pyramid

    C. rectangular prism

    D. cone

23. If a commercial jet travels 570 miles per hour, how many miles will it travel in 4 hours?

    A. 143 miles

    B. 1,140 miles

    C. 2,280 miles

    D. 2,850 miles

24. The number of students in Marilyn's school for each of four consecutive years is shown in the table below.

Year	Number of Students
1	212
2	226
3	240
4	254

    If the pattern continued, how many students would you expect to be accepted into the program in Year 5?

    A. 264

    B. 266

    C. 268

    D. 270

Go to next page

25. Teresa plans to set up a lemonade stand at a local fair. She will purchase 250 cans of lemonade for a total of $75 and will charge $2.50 for each can she sells. In addition to the cost of the lemonade, Teresa will need to pay $20 to set up the stand. Which of the following expressions could Teresa use to find out how much money she could make after expenses, for selling x cans of juice?

A. $2.5x - 75 - 20$

B. $x + 2.50 - 75 - 20$

C. $2.50 - 75 - \dfrac{20}{x}$

D. $2.5x(75 - 20)$

26. Ashaki joined her school's cross country team. As part of her training, she is going to increase the number of miles she runs every week by 2 miles. If she runs 21 miles the first week, how many miles will she run during the eighth week?

A. 29 miles

B. 31 miles

C. 35 miles

D. 37 miles

27. Megan is going on a field trip to Washington, D.C. The bus leaves her school at 5:30 a.m. It stops at a rest stop for 15 minutes and later stops for lunch for 1 hour. If the bus did not stop, it would have taken it 5½ hours to get to Washington, D.C. At what time did the bus arrive at its destination?

    A. 10:30 a.m.

    B. 11:00 a.m.

    C. 12:00 p.m.

    D. 12:15 p.m.

28. Figure *ABCDE* is a regular pentagon.

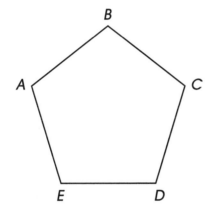

What is the measure, in degrees, of ∠*ABC*?

    A. 108°

    B. 120°

    C. 135°

    D. 180°

Go to next page

29. Beth scored 18, 18, 15, 18, 18, 24, 21, 20, 24, and 14 points during her first ten basketball games. What is her mean score?

   A. 10

   B. 18

   C. 19

   D. 21

30. Look at the clock shown below.

What is the approximate measure of the central angle shown?

   A. 3°

   B. 12°

   C. 30°

   D. 90°

31. A system of equations is shown below.

    $2x + 2y = 20$

    $2x - y = 14$

    What is the solution to the system of equations?

    A. $x = 4, y = 6$

    B. $x = 17, y = 20$

    C. $x = 8, y = 2$

    D. $x = 16, y = 4$

32. The perimeter of a triangle is 28. Two of its sides measure 12 and 8. What is the length of the remaining side?

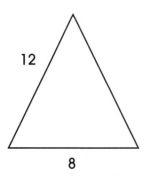

    A. 6

    B. 8

    C. 10

    D. 12

Go to next page

33. Look at the similar figures below.

For question 33, respond completely on your **Answer Document**. (4 points)

In your **Answer Document**, write a proportion that can be used to find the length of the larger rectangle. Solve the proportion to determine the length of the larger rectangle. Show your work or provide an explanation to support your answer. (4 points)

34. What is another way to express 250,000?

   A. 254

   B. 503

   C. 2.5×10^4

   D. 2.5×10^5

35. A clothing store marked all sweaters $\frac{1}{4}$ off the original price for a sale. Alex has a store coupon that is good for an additional discount of 10% off the sale price. She purchases a sweater that was originally priced at $45.00. If she also uses her discount coupon, what should be the cost of the sweater before the sales tax is added?

   A. $14.55

   B. $23.75

   C. $30.37

   D. $33.75

36. Which of these is not a function?

A.

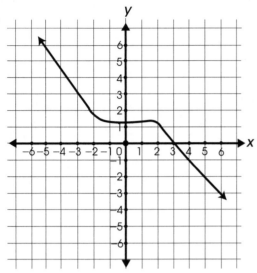

C.

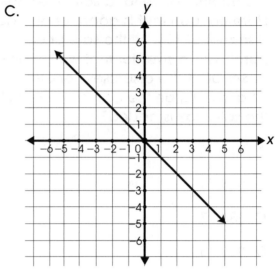

B.

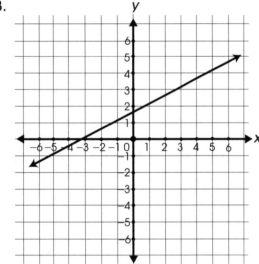

D.

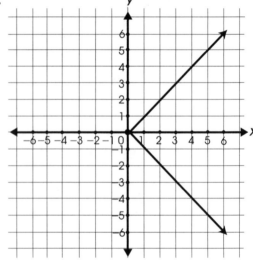

37. Steven is designing a mosaic. He is reflecting triangle TUV over the dashed diagonal line shown on the coordinate plane below to create triangle T'U'V'.

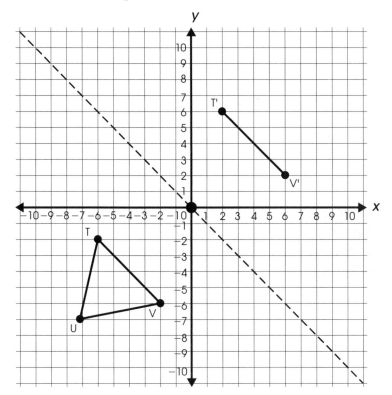

To complete his design, what should be the coordinates of U'?

A. (1, 1)

B. (7, 7)

C. (2, 6)

D. (6, 2)

Go to next page

38. The length of Kiera's driveway is $3\sqrt{7}$ feet. Which of the following numbers is closest to the length of her driveway?

    A. 6 feet

    B. 8 feet

    C. 12 feet

    D. 21 feet

39. Madeline earns $8.25 an hour babysitting her cousins during the 10 weeks of summer vacation. If she averages 12 hours per week, how much does Madeline earn during the summer?

    A. $82.50

    B. $99.00

    C. $825.00

    D. $990.00

Go to next page

40. The graph of line d is shown below. The slope of this line is 2.

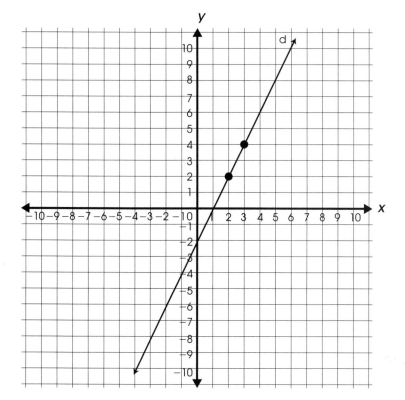

Which of the following is the slope of a line that is parallel to line d?

A. –2

B. 0

C. $\frac{1}{2}$

D. 2

41. Determine the volume of a cylinder with a radius of 3 inches and a height of 12 inches.

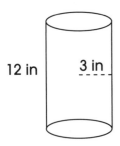

A. 108 cubic inches

B. 113 cubic inches

C. 226 cubic inches

D. 339 cubic inches

42. If $\angle ACB$ measures 45°, what is the measure, in degrees, of $\angle BCD$?

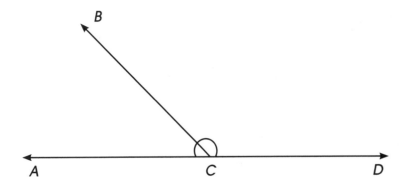

A. 75°

B. 90°

C. 135°

D. 180°

43. Which equation is equivalent to $6(x - 2) = 3(x + 1)$?

    A. $3x = -15$

    B. $3x = 15$

    C. $9x = -9$

    D. $9x = 9$

44. Which expression represents 530,000 written in scientific notation?

    A. 530×10^3

    B. 53×10^4

    C. 5.3×10^5

    D. $.53 \times 10^6$

Stop

Practice Test 2 Answer Explanations

1. B (Patterns, Functions, and Algebra: D)
Frankie has 30 baseball cards at the beginning of the week and he gives x away. So, you know the expression will begin with $30 - x$. Then Frankie's mother gives him more baseball cards (y). The entire expression should be $30 - x + y$.

2. C (Data Analysis and Probability: I)
There are six sections in the spinner, so the denominator will be 6. Two of these sections have a 2, so the probability is $\frac{2}{6}$, or $\frac{1}{3}$.

3. D (Number Sense: E)
To answer this question, you need to determine the value of each answer choice. Answer choice A, the square root of 196, is 14. Answer choice B, 3 times the square root of 12, is approximately 10. Answer choice C, 2 raised to the fourth power, is 16. And, answer choice D, 3 raised to the third power, is 27. Answer choice D is the correct answer.

4. D (Patterns, Functions, and Algebra: D)
The expression $4(x + 2y) + 2(3x - y) - (x + y)$ can be simplified like this:

$4x + 8y + 6x - 2y - x - y$. Then combine like terms: $9x + 5y$

5. (Number Sense: G)
To solve this problem, you first need to determine the 35% discount. Multiply .35 by $195.99, the price of the bike before the discount. Then deduct this amount ($68.60) from $195.99 to get $127.39.

6. A (Data Analysis and Probability: B)
A bar graph is best to display this data, since it would clearly show that most students who speak a second language speak Spanish. A line graph shows the relationship between two variables, and there is only one variable here. The other answer choices would not display this type of data effectively.

7.   (Data Analysis and Probability: C)

Sample answer: $200 + 225 + 240 + 240 + 280 + 375 + 400 = 1,960$

$1,960 \div 7 \div 280$. This is the mean.

The mode is 240 and the median is 240.

Management would use the mean in an argument against pay raises because that is the highest measure, and the labor union could use either the mode or median in an argument for pay raises because either one is the lowest measure.

8.   B   (Data Analysis and Probability: H)

If you put the main dishes in a vertical line—chicken, fish, and roast beef—and list the side dishes to the right of this, you'll see that for each main dish, there are five possible combinations of side dishes. There are three main dishes, so there are 15 choices.

chicken	salad
fish	green beans
roast beef	baked potatoes
	mashed potatoes
	apple sauce

9.   B   (Data Analysis and Probability: I)

The denominator is 30 since this is how many marbles are in the bag. There are 5 red marbles in the bag. So the probability of pulling out a red marble is $\frac{5}{30}$, which reduces to $\frac{1}{6}$.

10.   B   (Number Sense: D)

Point Q is the closest to 4.5, the approximate square root of 20. You don't have to know the exact value of $\sqrt{20}$, only that it must be between $\sqrt{16}$ and $\sqrt{25}$, or between 4 and 5.

11. (Measurement: D)

Sample answer: To solve this problem, set up a proportion: $\frac{94}{74} = \frac{50}{x}$. Then, solve the proportion by cross-multiplying:

$94x = 3,700$

Divide each side of the equation by 94.

$$\frac{94x}{94} = \frac{3,700}{94}$$

$x = 39$ feet

12. (Measurement: B)

Sample answer: For a cylinder, $V = \pi r^2 h$

Capacity found by increasing diameter 1 inch:

Since $h = 4$, and $d = 4$ (or $r = 2$),

$V = (3.14) \times 2^2 \times 4$

$V = (3.14) \times 4 \times 4$

$V = 50.24$ cubic inches

Capacity found by increasing height 1 inch:

Since $h = 5$, $d = 3$ (or $r = 1.5$),

$V = (3.14) \times 1.5^2 \times 5$

$V = 3.14 \times 2.25 \times 5$

$V = 35.33$ cubic inches

$50.25 - 35.33 = 14.9$

So the difference between increasing the diameter 1 inch and increasing the height 1 inch is 14.9 cubic inches.

13. C   (Geometry and Spatial Sense: D)
A rectangle has two pairs of parallel lines. Answer choice C (6, 6) is the correct answer.

14. A   (Geometry and Spatial Sense: A)
Answer choice A shows an acute triangle, a triangle with all angles less than 90 degrees.

15. D   (Geometry and Spatial Sense: A)
A parallelogram has two sets of congruent parallel sides, and opposite angles are congruent. The figures in answer choices A, B, and C meet these criteria because squares and rectangles are special types of parallelograms. Answer choice D is the only one that doesn't.

16. Sample Answer: (Number Sense: G)
To find the number of people employed in manufacturing jobs, multiply 131,000,000 by 13% or .13. The answer is 17 million.

17. C   **(Measurement: C)**
Use $V = lwh$. If you multiply 12 by 6 and then multiply that answer by 4, you get 288.

18. Sample answer: **(Data Analysis and Probability: D)**
To find the mean, you need to add all of the numbers (total = 1,422) and divide by the number of months (7). The answer is 203.

19. Sample answer: **(Patterns, Functions, and Algebra: D)**
Melanie worked 40 hours for which she earned $8 per hour. She earned $320 for the 40 hours. Then she worked 8 hours of overtime, for which she is paid $12 per hour. She earned $96 in overtime. If you add $320 + $96, the answer is $416.

20. A   **(Patterns, Functions, and Algebra: F)**
A linear function graphs as one straight line.

21. B   **(Data Analysis and Probability: C)**
An average of 85 for 5 tests means the sum of the five tests must equal $5 \times 85 = 425$. So $80 + 83 + 90 + 92 + x = 425$, and $x = 80$.

22. A   **(Geometry and Spatial Sense: E)**
The base and top of this net are triangles and the sides are rectangles; therefore, it's a triangular prism.

23. C   **(Patterns, Functions, and Algebra: J)**
If you multiply 570 by 4, the answer is 2,280.

24. C   **(Patterns, Functions, and Algebra: A)**
The numbers are increasing by the same amount (14) each year. Add this amount onto the enrollment for Year 4 to get the expected enrollment for year 5, which is 268.

25. A   **(Patterns, Functions, and Algebra: D)**
The variable in this problem is x, the number of cans of lemonade Teresa sells. Teresa will charge $2.50 for each can, so she will collect $2.5x$ dollars, but she will have to subtract her costs ($75 for the lemonade and $20 for the stand). The best expression is $2.5x - 75 - 20$.

26. C **(Patterns, Functions, and Algebra: A)**

Begin with the number 21, the number of miles Ashaki runs during the first week. Then, add 2 to this number for each week until you get to the eighth week. Remember that week 1 is 21 miles.

27. D **(Measurement: F)**

If the bus didn't stop, it would have reached Washington, D.C., at 11:00 a.m. However, it stopped for an hour and 15 minutes, so it reached its destination at 12:15 p.m.

28. A **(Measurement: E)**

Each angle in a regular pentagon measures 108°.

29. C **(Data Analysis and Probability: D)**

When you add up Beth's scores, the answer is 190. When you divide this by 10—the number of games—the answer is 19.

30. D **(Measurement: C)**

The measure of a circle is 360°. This clock is divided into 12 sections of 30° each, and the central angle is made up of three sections, so the correct answer is 90°.

31. C **(Patterns, Functions, and Algebra: D)**

Check to see whether each answer choice is a solution to both equations (that is, makes them true). If you substitute 8 for x and 2 for y, you'll see that both equations are correct.

32. B **(Measurement: C)**

The sum of the three sides equals 28, so you need to add 12 and 8 and subtract this number from 28. The third side is 8.

33. Sample answer: **(Measurement: D)**

Since the rectangles are similar, their sides must be proportional. If you compare their heights, the ratio is 2:4, or 1:2. This must be the proportion for the lengths as well, so $\frac{3}{x} = \frac{1}{2}$, or $x = 6$, the length of the second rectangle.

34. D **(Number Sense: A)**

You must move the decimal over to the left 5 places so that it is between the first and second digits. So 5 equals the exponent.

35. C   (Number Sense: G)

First determine the sale price: $\frac{1}{4}$ or 25 percent of $45 equals $11.25. $45.00 − $11.25 = $33.75. The sale price is $33.75. Then take 10% off this price: $33.75 − $3.38 = $30.37.

36. D   (Patterns, Functions, and Algebra: E)

The graph in answer choice D fails the vertical line test, so it is not a function.

37. B   (Geometry and Spatial Sense: I)

Reflection is a mirror image. Answer choice A would make only a translation of triangle TUV; and answer choices C and D give the coordinates of points T′ and V′, respectively. If the coordinates of point U′ were (7, 7), triangle T′U′V′ would be a reflection, so answer choice B is correct.

38. B   (Numbers, Number Sense, and Operations: I)

If $3\sqrt{7} = 6$, answer choice A, then $\sqrt{7} = 2$, but since $\sqrt{4} = 2, 6$ is too low. If $3\sqrt{7} = 12$, answer choice C, then $\sqrt{7} = 4$, but you know that $\sqrt{16} = 4$, so 12 is too high, and thus 21, answer choice D would also be too high. If you check answer choice B, 8, then $3\sqrt{7} = 8$, or $\sqrt{7} = \frac{8}{3}$, which is just about right.

39. D   (Measurement: F)

To determine how much money Madeline earns during the summer, multiply her hourly wage, $8.25 by 12, the number of hours she works per week. Then multiply this amount by 10, the number of weeks she works during the summer.

40. D   (Geometry and Spatial Sense: D)

Parallel lines have the same slope, so the answer is 2.

41. D   (Geometry and Spatial Sense: D)

For a cylinder, $V = \pi r^2 h$. If you plug the correct amounts into the formula, it looks like this: $V = 3.14 \times 9 \times 12 = 339$.

42. C   (Geometry and Spatial Sense: I)

These angles are supplementary; therefore, they add up to 180°. To find the answer, subtract the value of the given angle, 45°, from 180°.

43. B **(Patterns, Functions and Algebra: F)**

$6(x - 2) = 3(x + 1)$

$6x - 12 = 3x + 3$ distribute the numbers in front of the parentheses to the terms inside

$6x = 3x + 15$ add 12 to each side of the equation

$3x = 15$ subtract 3x from each side of the equation

44. C **(Number, Number Sense and Operations: A)**

Take the number 530,000 and move the decimal point to the left 5 places, which is 5. The number becomes 5.3 times 10 raised to the 5th power or 5.3×10^5

Optional Graph Paper

NOTHING ON THIS PAPER WILL BE SCORED

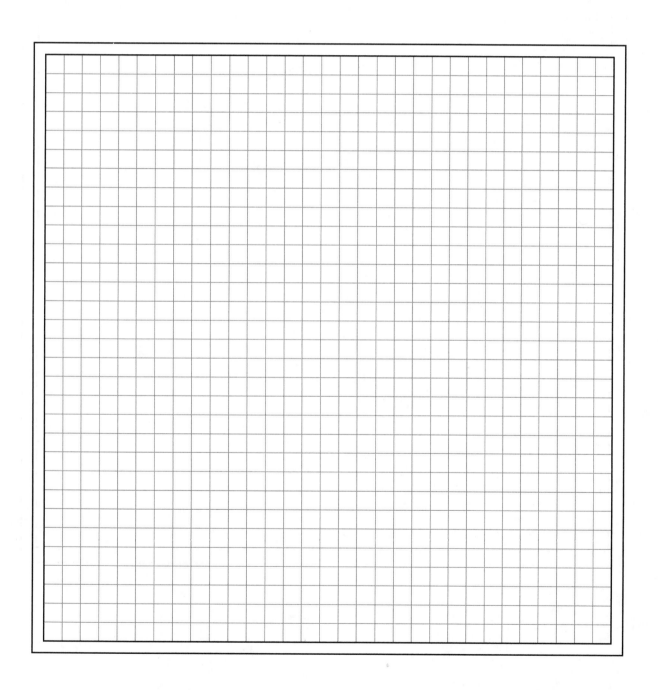

ANSWER DOCUMENT

1. Write your response to question 1 in the space below.

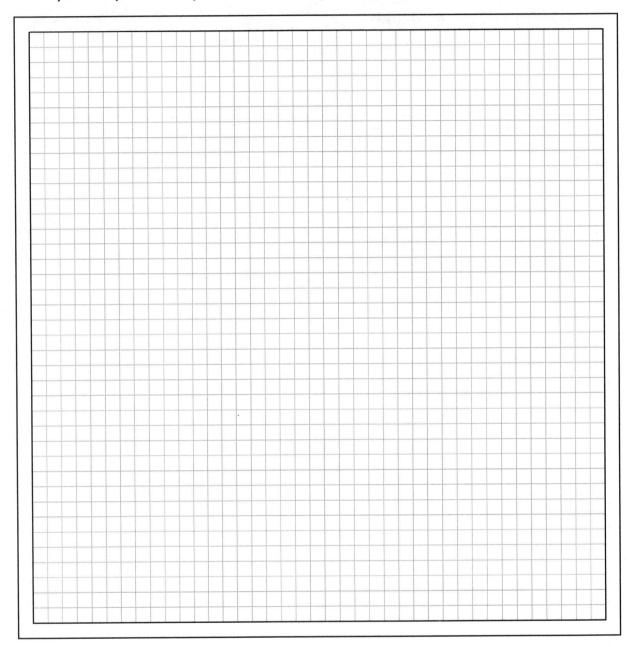

2. Ⓐ   Ⓑ   Ⓒ   Ⓓ

3. Ⓐ   Ⓑ   Ⓒ   Ⓓ

4. Write your response to question 4 in the space below.

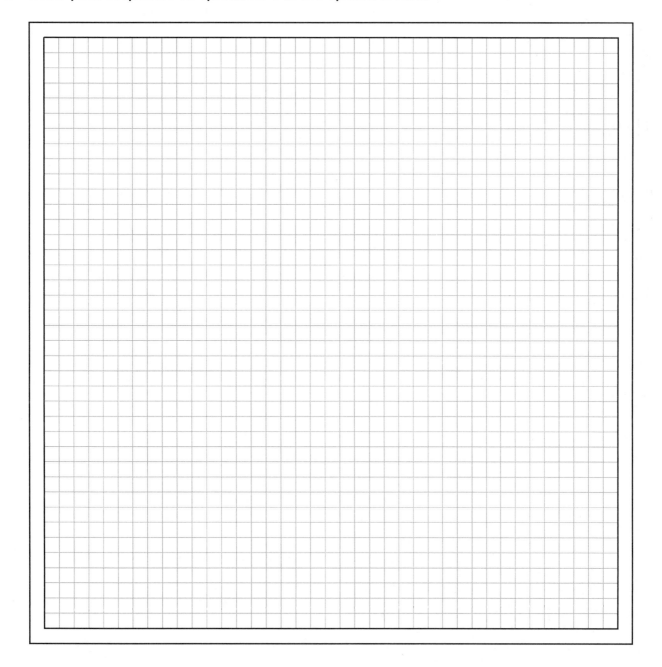

5. Ⓐ Ⓑ Ⓒ Ⓓ

6. Ⓐ Ⓑ Ⓒ Ⓓ

7. Ⓐ Ⓑ Ⓒ Ⓓ

8. Ⓐ Ⓑ Ⓒ Ⓓ

9. Ⓐ Ⓑ Ⓒ Ⓓ

10. Ⓐ Ⓑ Ⓒ Ⓓ

11. Ⓐ Ⓑ Ⓒ Ⓓ

12. Ⓐ Ⓑ Ⓒ Ⓓ

13. Ⓐ Ⓑ Ⓒ Ⓓ

14. Ⓐ Ⓑ Ⓒ Ⓓ

15. Ⓐ Ⓑ Ⓒ Ⓓ

16. Ⓐ Ⓑ Ⓒ Ⓓ

17. Write your response to question 17 in the space below.

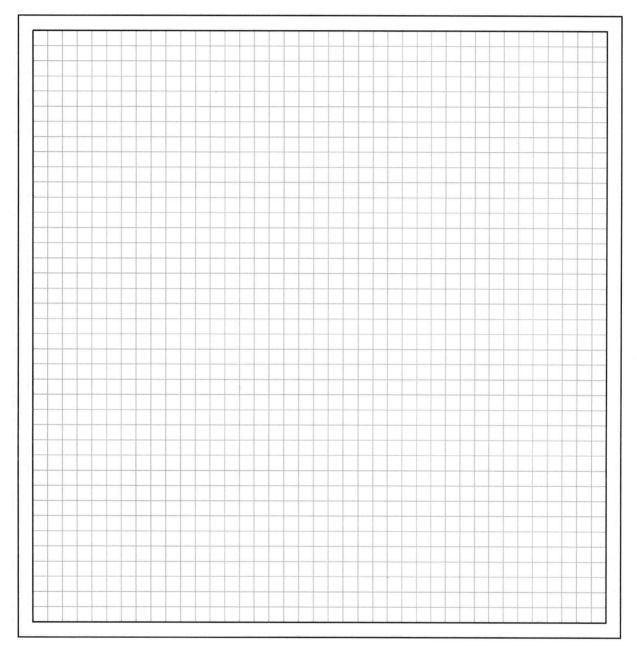

18. Ⓐ   Ⓑ   Ⓒ   Ⓓ

19. Write your response to question 19 in the space below.

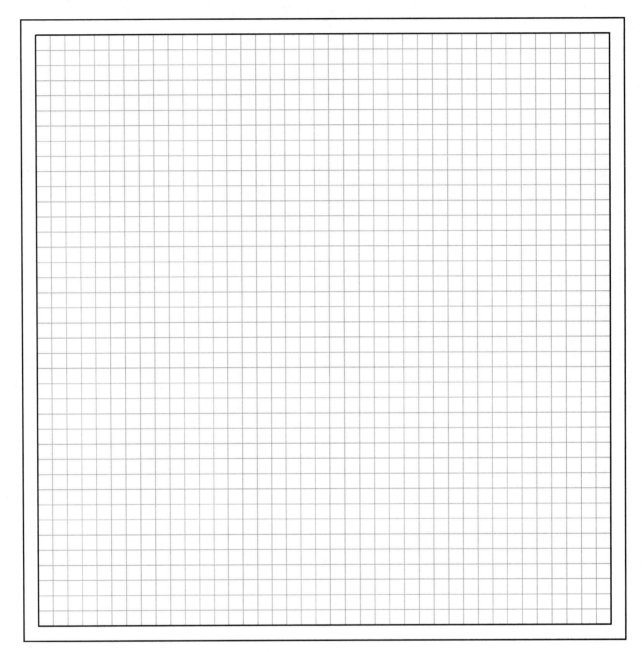

20. Ⓐ   Ⓑ   Ⓒ   Ⓓ

21. Ⓐ   Ⓑ   Ⓒ   Ⓓ

22. Ⓐ   Ⓑ   Ⓒ   Ⓓ

23. Ⓐ   Ⓑ   Ⓒ   Ⓓ

24. Ⓐ   Ⓑ   Ⓒ   Ⓓ

25. Ⓐ   Ⓑ   Ⓒ   Ⓓ

26. Ⓐ   Ⓑ   Ⓒ   Ⓓ

27. Ⓐ   Ⓑ   Ⓒ   Ⓓ

28. Write your response to question 28 in the space below.

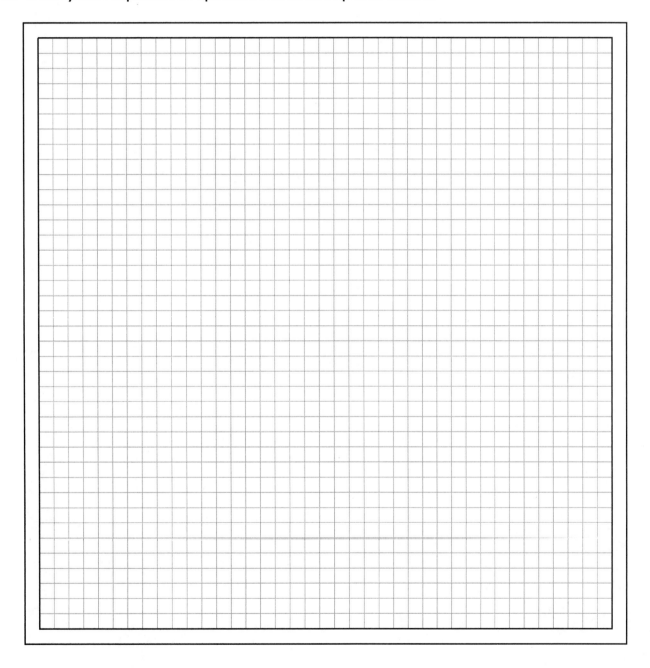

29. Ⓐ   Ⓑ   Ⓒ   Ⓓ

30. Ⓐ   Ⓑ   Ⓒ   Ⓓ

31. Ⓐ   Ⓑ   Ⓒ   Ⓓ

32. Ⓐ   Ⓑ   Ⓒ   Ⓓ

33. Ⓐ   Ⓑ   Ⓒ   Ⓓ

34. Ⓐ   Ⓑ   Ⓒ   Ⓓ

35. Write your response to question 35 in the space below.

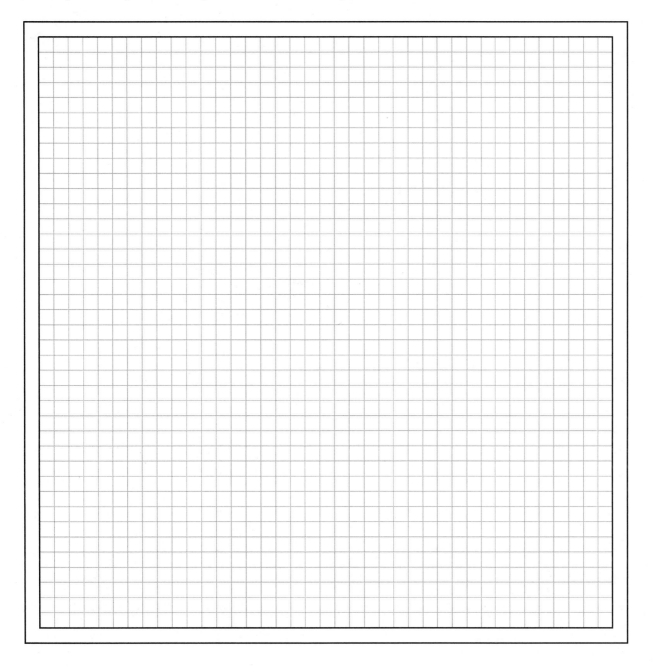

36. Ⓐ Ⓑ Ⓒ Ⓓ

37. Ⓐ Ⓑ Ⓒ Ⓓ

38. Ⓐ Ⓑ Ⓒ Ⓓ

39. Ⓐ Ⓑ Ⓒ Ⓓ

40. Ⓐ   Ⓑ   Ⓒ   Ⓓ

41. Ⓐ   Ⓑ   Ⓒ   Ⓓ

42. Ⓐ   Ⓑ   Ⓒ   Ⓓ

43. Ⓐ   Ⓑ   Ⓒ   Ⓓ

44. Ⓐ   Ⓑ   Ⓒ   Ⓓ

Optional Graph Paper

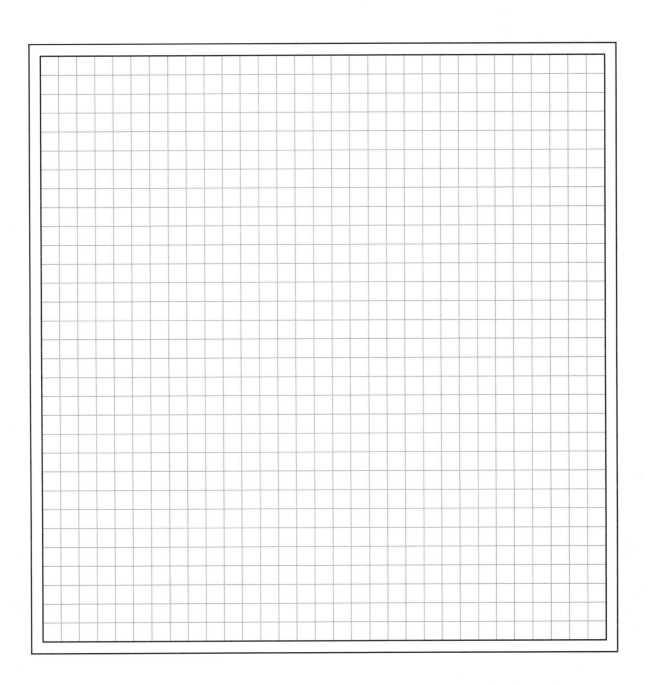

ANSWER DOCUMENT

1. Ⓐ Ⓑ Ⓒ Ⓓ

2. Ⓐ Ⓑ Ⓒ Ⓓ

3. Ⓐ Ⓑ Ⓒ Ⓓ

4. Ⓐ Ⓑ Ⓒ Ⓓ

5. Write your response to question 5 in the space below.

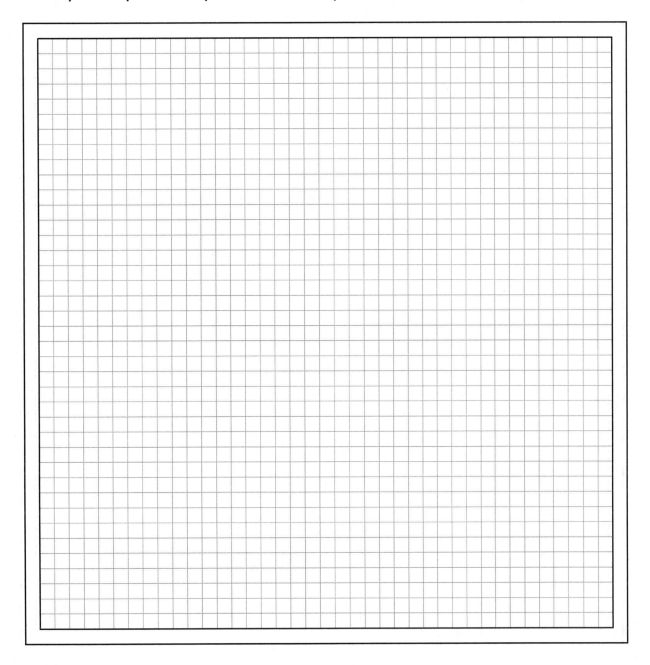

6. Ⓐ   Ⓑ   Ⓒ   Ⓓ

7. Write your response to question 7 in the space below.

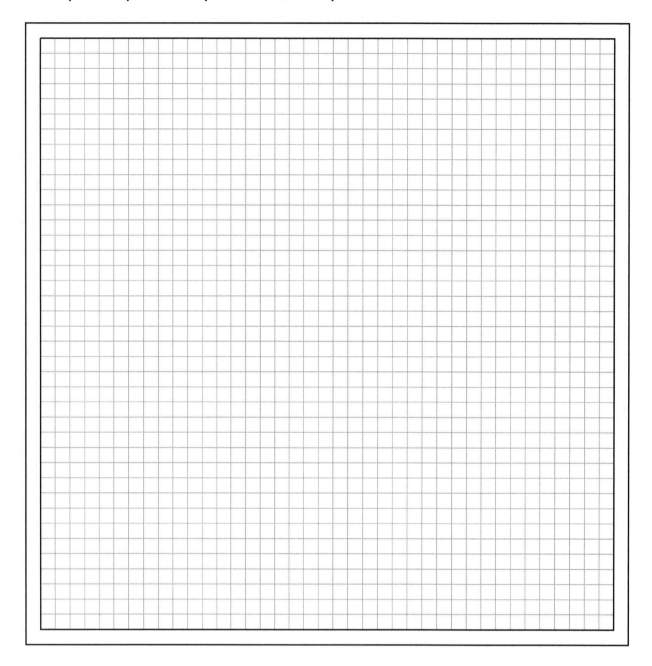

8. Ⓐ Ⓑ Ⓒ Ⓓ

9. Ⓐ Ⓑ Ⓒ Ⓓ

10. Ⓐ Ⓑ Ⓒ Ⓓ

11. Write your response to question 11 in the space below.

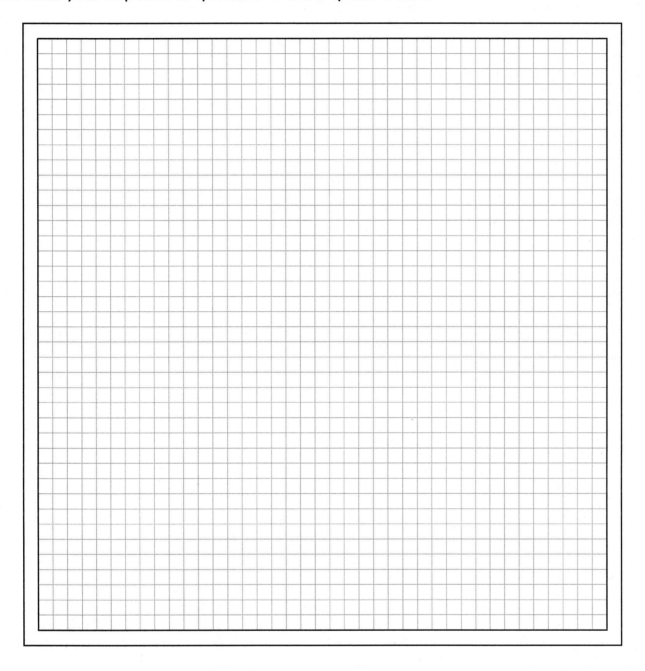

12. Write your response to question 12 in the space below.

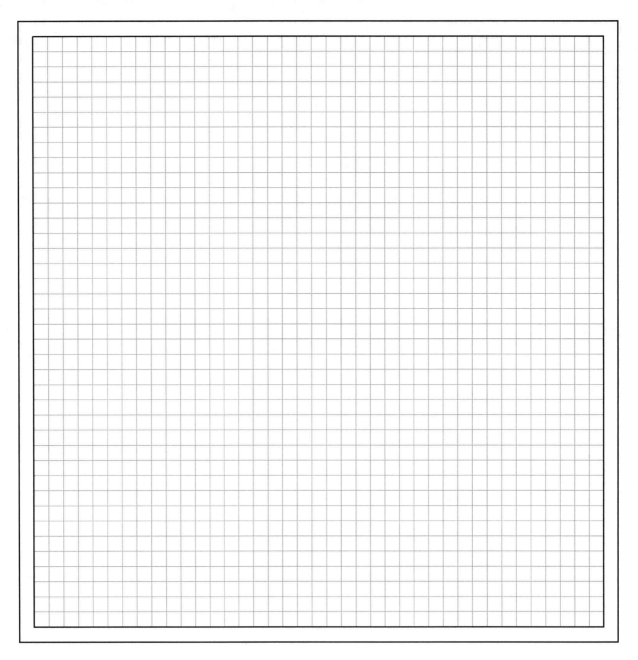

13. Ⓐ   Ⓑ   Ⓒ   Ⓓ

14. Ⓐ   Ⓑ   Ⓒ   Ⓓ

15. Ⓐ   Ⓑ   Ⓒ   Ⓓ

16. Write your response to question 16 in the space below.

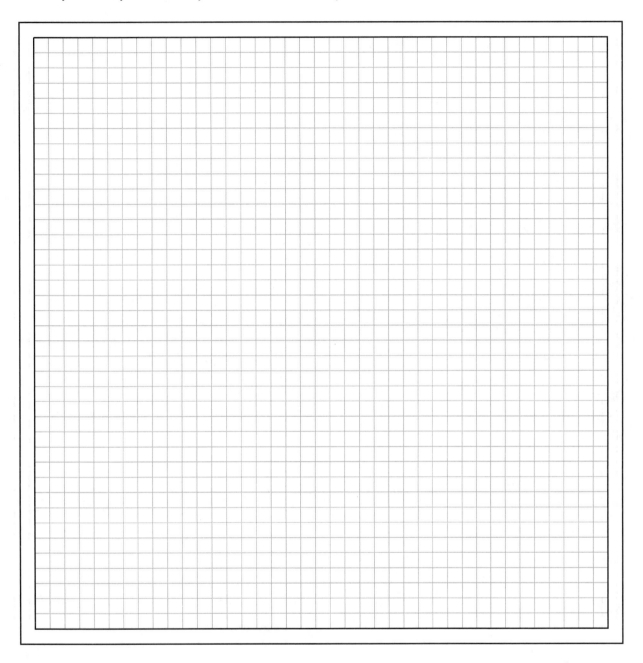

17. Ⓐ　Ⓑ　Ⓒ　Ⓓ

18. Write your response to question 18 in the space below.

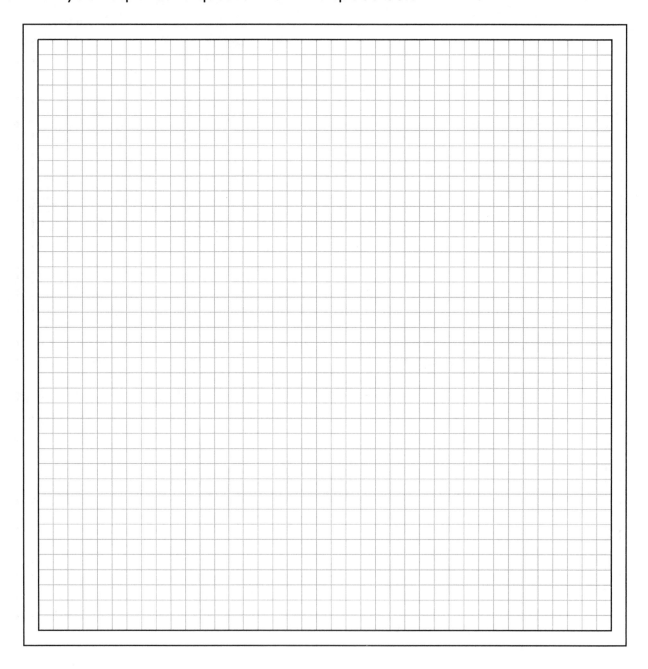

19. Write your response to question 19 in the space below.

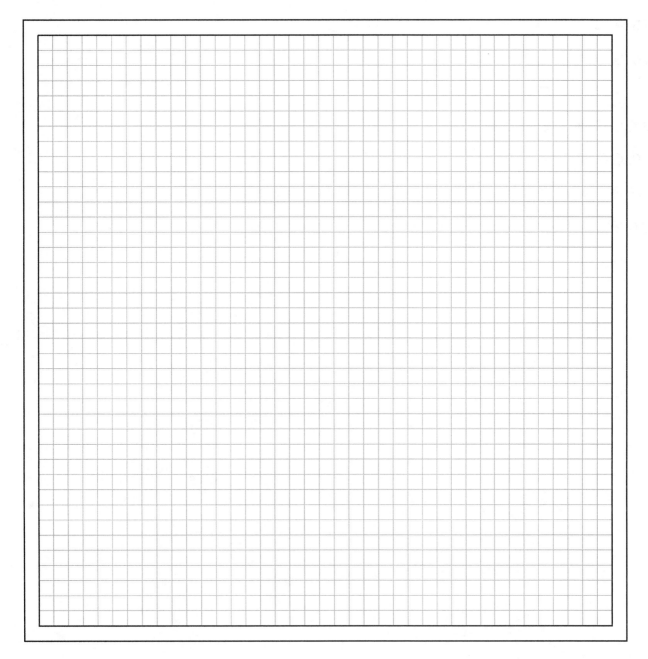

20. Ⓐ   Ⓑ   Ⓒ   Ⓓ

21. Ⓐ   Ⓑ   Ⓒ   Ⓓ

22. Ⓐ   Ⓑ   Ⓒ   Ⓓ

23. Ⓐ   Ⓑ   Ⓒ   Ⓓ

24. Ⓐ   Ⓑ   Ⓒ   Ⓓ

25. Ⓐ   Ⓑ   Ⓒ   Ⓓ

26. Ⓐ   Ⓑ   Ⓒ   Ⓓ

27. Ⓐ   Ⓑ   Ⓒ   Ⓓ

28. Ⓐ   Ⓑ   Ⓒ   Ⓓ

29. Ⓐ   Ⓑ   Ⓒ   Ⓓ

30. Ⓐ   Ⓑ   Ⓒ   Ⓓ

31. Ⓐ   Ⓑ   Ⓒ   Ⓓ

32. Ⓐ   Ⓑ   Ⓒ   Ⓓ

33. Write your response to question 33 in the space below.

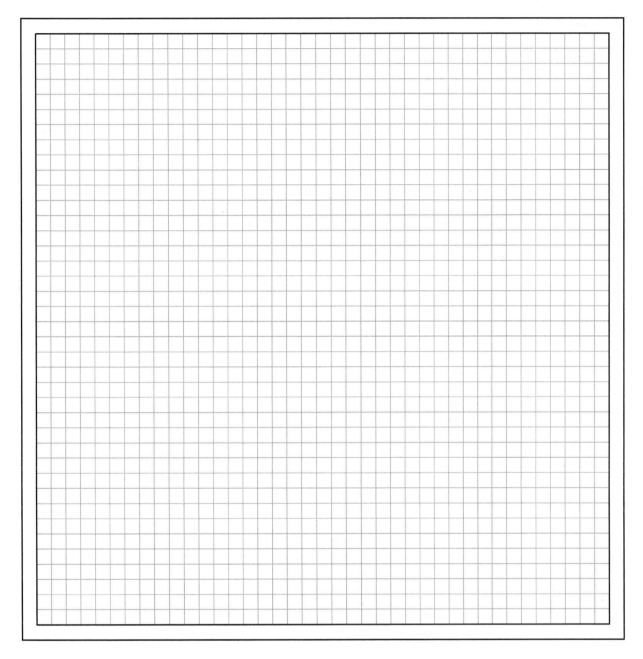

34. Ⓐ   Ⓑ   Ⓒ   Ⓓ

35. Ⓐ   Ⓑ   Ⓒ   Ⓓ

36. Ⓐ   Ⓑ   Ⓒ   Ⓓ

37. Ⓐ   Ⓑ   Ⓒ   Ⓓ

38. Ⓐ   Ⓑ   Ⓒ   Ⓓ

39. Ⓐ   Ⓑ   Ⓒ   Ⓓ

40. Ⓐ   Ⓑ   Ⓒ   Ⓓ

41. Ⓐ   Ⓑ   Ⓒ   Ⓓ

42. Ⓐ   Ⓑ   Ⓒ   Ⓓ

43. Ⓐ   Ⓑ   Ⓒ   Ⓓ

44. Ⓐ   Ⓑ   Ⓒ   Ⓓ

OGT Mathematics
Index

Index

A

Absolute value, 13
Accommodations, 2
Acute angles, 108
Acute triangles, 112
Addition, of powers, 40–41
Adjacent angles, 109
Algebraic equations, 173–177, 196
Algebraic expressions, 172–173
Angles, 108–110, 151–152
Area, 154–156

B

Bar graphs, 78–79
Bases, 39
Bias, 86
Box-and-whisker plots, 84–85

C

Calculator use
    powers, 20
    scientific notation, 21
    square root, 23
Central angles, 151–152
Circle graphs, 79–80
Circles
    area, 155
    central angles in, 151–152
    circumference, 150–151
    description, 101
Circumference, 150–151
Clustering, 35
Combinations, 62
Common factors, 17
Complementary angles, 109
Cones, 103, 157
Congruent figures, 99–100
Conversions
    decimal into percent, 17
    percent into decimal, 17
    percent into fraction, 17
Coordinate planes, 124–129
Coordinates, 124–125, 182
Cube of number, 19, 40
Cubes, 102
Cylinders, 103, 157, 159

D

Decimals, 15–16, 17
Denominators, 13
Differential, 192
Disabled students, 2
Discounts, 44
Division, of powers, 41

E

Edges, 102
Endpoints, 107
English language learners (ELL), 2
Equations, 173–177, 196
Equilateral triangles, 112
Equivalent fractions, 14–15
Equivalent numbers, 13
Estimation, 34–36
Exponents, 19, 39
Expressions, 172–173

F

Faces, 102
First quartile, 85
Fractions, 13–15, 17
Front-end estimation, 36
Functions, 183–186

G

Geometric figures, 99–104
Graphs, 78–80

H

Hexagons, 101
Hypotenuse, 112

I

Inequalities, 177–178
Integers, 12
Interest, 45
Inverse operation, 22
Inverse relationships, 192
Irrational numbers, 12
Isosceles triangles, 112

L

Legs, 112
Linear equations, 182–183
Linear functions, 186
Line graphs, 78
Lines, 107, 109–110, 132
Line segments, 107

M

Mean, 64
Measures of central tendency, 58
Median, 64
Mixed numbers, 15, 16
Mode, 64
Money problems, 43–45, 160
Multiplication
    of fractions, 14
    of powers, 41
Multi-step problems, 160

N
Nets, 131–132
Numbers, types of, 12
Numerators, 13

O
Obtuse angles, 108
Obtuse triangles, 113
Octagons, 102
Ohio Graduation Test (OGT)
    about, 1
    accommodations, 2
    overview of, 3–4
    standards, 5–8
    study tips, 3
    test-taking tips, 9–10
    when/where given, 2
Opposites, 12
Origin, 124

P
Parabola, 195
Parallel lines, 107, 110
Parallelograms, 101, 155
Patterns, 181
Pentagons, 101
Percents, 16–17
Perimeter, 149–150
Perpendicular lines, 107
Pi (π), 150
Pie charts or graphs, 79–80
Plane figures
    nets, 131–132
    types of, 100–102
Point of intersection, 107
Polygons, 102
Polyhedrons, 104
Polynomials, 194
Powers, 19–20, 39–41
Principal, 45
Prisms
    description, 103
    surface area, 159
    volume, 157, 158
Probability, 57, 58–59
Proportions, 38–39
Pyramids, 103, 158
Pythagorean theorem, 113–114

Quadratic equations, 196
Quadratic functions, 194–195

R
Radicals, 22–23
Radicands, 23
Radius, 151
Range, 65
Rate of change, 192–193

Rational numbers, 12
Ratios, 38
Rays, 107
Real numbers, 12
Rectangles, 100, 146, 154
Rectangular solids, 102, 157, 159
Reducing fractions, 17
Reflection, 129
Reflex angles, 108
Rhombuses, 101
Right angles, 108
Right circular cones, 103
Right circular cylinders, 103, 159
Right triangles, 112
Rise-over-run formula, 132
Rotation, 129
Rounding, 34–35

S
Sale prices, 44
Sales tax, 45
Sampling methods, 86
Scalene triangles, 112
Scatter plats, 83–84
Scientific notation, 20–22
Second quartile, 85
Similar figures, 146–147
Slope, 132
Special education students, 2
Spheres, 103, 158
Square of number, 19, 20, 39
Square pyramids, 103, 158
Square roots, 22
Squares, 100
Standards, 5–8
Stem-and-leaf plots, 85
Straight angles, 108
Subtraction, of powers, 40–41
Supplementary angles, 109
Surface area, 159
System of equations, 175–177

T
Third quartile, 85
Three-dimensional figures
    surface area, 159
    types of, 102–104
    volume, 157–159
Transformations, 128–129
Translation, 129
Transversals, 110
Trapezoids, 101, 155
Tree diagrams, 62
Triangles
    area, 155
    description, 101, 111
    Pythagorean theorem, 113–114
    similar, 146

types of, 111–113
Triangular prisms, 103

V

Variables, 172
Venn diagrams, 80
Vertex (vertices)
    definition, 108
    three-dimensional figures, 102
    triangles, 111
Vertical angles, 110

Vertical line test, 184–185
Volume, 157–159

X

x-axis, 124
x-intercept, 132

Y

y-axis, 124
y-intercept, 132

NOTES

NOTES

NOTES

NOTES

NOTES

NOTES